HOOPS HEAVEN

NAISMITH MEMORIAL
BASKETBALL HALL OF FAME
50th
ANNIVERSARY
1959 - 2009

ASCEND BOOKS

www.ascendbooks.com

Requests for permission should be addressed to Ascend Books, LLC, Attn: Rights and Permissions Department, 7015 College Blvd., Suite 600, Overland Park, KS 66211.

10 9 8 7 6 5 4 3 2 1

Printed in the United States of America

ISBN-13: 978-0-9817166-8-8

ISBN-10: 0-9817166-8-7

Library of Congress Cataloging-in-Publications Data Available Upon Request

Ascend Books, LLC

Publisher: Bob Snodgrass

Executive Editor: Lee Stuart

Chief Financial Officer: John Vandewalle

Sponsorship and Corporate Sales: Larry Krakow, Lenny Cohen, and Jennifer Wonderly

Publication Coordinator: Whitney Barnes

Publicity: Kerry Comiskey

Book Design: Randy Lackey, The Covington Group

Special Thanks to

www.ascendbooks.com

HOOPS

NAISMITH MEMORIAL
BASKETBALL HALL OF FAME
50th
ANNIVERSARY
1959-2009

HEAVEN

Commemorating the 50th Anniversary of the
Naismith Memorial Basketball Hall of Fame

TABLE OF CONTENTS

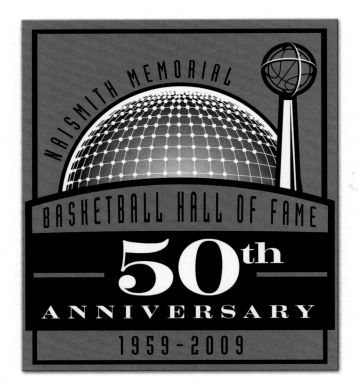

NAISMITH MEMORIAL
BASKETBALL HALL OF FAME
50th
ANNIVERSARY
1959-2009

PUBLISHER'S NOTE

We are proud to be selected as the publisher for this official commemorative book. *Hoops Heaven* is a book of celebration, a book of tribute, and a book of reflection. *Hoops Heaven* is not a chronological re-counting of the history of the game – nor is it a reference manual detailing every great player or coach. It is a one-of-a-kind tribute to just some of the significant people, moments, and ideas that have shaped the game we love.

Congratulations to the players, coaches, executives, and fans who have worked to perpetuate – and preserve – this wonderful game for more than 100 years.

Bob Snodgrass, Publisher – Ascend Books

Lee Stuart, Executive Editor – Ascend Books

FOREWORD

Hall of Famers describe what being members of basketball's most exclusive club means to them

The Hall of Fame is sacred. It's sacred for all it brings—the people and the values of those people …all the people who have been so significant in our society. Now to join them – there is no greater honor that has been bestowed upon me.

Jim Calhoun, Class of 2005

Usually, you think about getting in the Hall of Fame as a player, but I only averaged 2.5 points per game, so the only way I was going to get in was as a coach … being elected to the Hall of Fame is a dream come true.

Al McGuire, Class of 1992

Enshrinement into the Basketball Hall of Fame is one of those career-defining honors. I played for so many years and with so many other great players and for four great coaches. Sometimes I begin to forget, but the Hall of Fame reminds me that every memory and every moment was real.

Bob Cousy, Class of 1971

The Basketball Hall of Fame has some pretty elite company in there. I am thrilled that the basketball part of my life was good enough to get me on that team.

Larry Bird, Class of 1998

Are you kidding me? Getting into the Hall of Fame is like the equivalent of calling a game with all the legends. I can see me on the sidelines now. Bill Russell grabs the rebound, passes ahead to Magic. Magic at half-court. Dr. J on the wing. Magic flips a no-look pass to Michael Jordan. Dippsy-do-dunkaroo! And my man on the sidelines? That's right. The General himself. Bobby Knight, Baby. Awesome with a capital A!

Dick Vitale, Class of 2008

What makes the Hall of Fame so special for a coach is that you really feel like all the players you coached and the leaders you coached with share the honor with you. That means the world to me.

Jody Conradt, Class of 1998

I never thought about the Hall of Fame coming up as a young coach. I did think about working hard, getting better every day. I still do to this day and I think being inducted into the Hall of Fame gives my approach legitimacy. The Hall of Fame if nothing else is about hard work and performing to the best of your ability.

Pat Summitt, Class of 2000

The Basketball Hall of Fame represents the best the game ever produced.

Jerry Colangelo, Class of 2004

I spent my entire life in basketball. I am proud to say that the work I did was worthy of the Basketball Hall of Fame. That is a legacy I hope lasts forever.

Dave Gavitt, Class of 2006

Getting the call to go into the Basketball Hall of Fame was one of the highlights of my career. I gave so much of myself to the game and I appreciate the honor and esteem that comes with being called a Hall of Famer.

Earl Lloyd, Class of 2003

There's nothing like being in the Hall of Fame. Basketball has been my life – the game my religion, the gym my church. You cannot express in words what it means or feels like to be enshrined in the Basketball Hall of Fame. Until you've experienced it … it's beyond comprehension.

Bill Walton, Class of 1993

I am proud to know that the pioneering work I did for women's basketball and women's sports continues to matter. Being recognized in the Hall of Fame ensures that a legacy for all women – not just my legacy or Pat Summitt's or Margaret Wade's – will live forever.

Cathy Rush, Class of 2008

At Georgetown, we always talked about a brotherhood. And I was part of one of the great basketball brotherhoods in history. Now to be part of the Hall of Fame … I feel like I joined an even bigger family with even greater parts.

Patrick Ewing, Class of 2008

Growing up in Louisiana, there was never any thought of a future that might include an honor like the Basketball Hall of Fame. Yet here I am after all these years … I guess all the hard work and sweat … pouring everything you have into one single objective … really does pay off.

Joe Dumars, Class of 2006

A Special Dedication by Pat Riley

It was a Friday, 11:50 a.m., April 3, 2008. The day after we just got our tails whipped by the New Orleans Hornets. I was watching video in my office from that nightmare of a game, preparing for practice and contemplating my coaching career while going through what was becoming the worst season in my 25 years of coaching. As I was watching Chris Paul lobbing passes to Tyson Chandler again and again for dunks, I received an expected but ominous phone call from Basketball Hall of Fame President & CEO John Doleva. He was calling to inform me that I had just been selected as the newest member of the Naismith Memorial Basketball Hall of Fame. **Pat Riley … Hall of Famer?**

I was stunned to silence and immediately dropped the phone, put my head in my hands, and wept. My mind flooded with images of my father. This was an honor I know my late father, Lee, would have been so proud of. An honor that I felt all along was the one gift I could give him that would make him smile. I wished I could get on the phone to Heaven and let him know how proud I was to have been his son. But I felt at that moment - you know those precious moments that are frozen in time - that yes, he did know of that pride. I COULD FEEL IT as the tears streamed down my face. I felt his warm embrace. Believe me when I say nothing quite

prepares you for this kind of emotion; it comes so quickly and never leaves.

There is a poignant quote that I used for many years: "YOU DON'T MERELY WANT TO BE CONSIDERED THE BEST OF THE BEST, YOU WANT TO BE CONSIDERED THE ONLY ONE WHO DOES WHAT YOU DO…THERE IS NOTHING WRONG WITH SEPARATING YOURSELF FROM THE PACK…TO REACH OUT AND UP…BECOME UNIQUE…AND LEAVE FOOTPRINTS IN THE SAND FOR OTHERS TO FOLLOW." I have become, along with so many others recognized in this light, a Hall of Famer and it feels as if my professional life has been stamped with a seal of approval from the greatest the game of basketball has ever known.

The official announcement of the Hall of Fame Class of 2008 came at the NCAA Final Four. As Chris – my wife of 38 years – and I traveled to San Antonio, Texas, where the press conference was to take place, we began to reflect back on all those times,

P at Riley led multiple teams to greatness.

places, and people where this glorious, wonderful, crazy journey dependent on a game connected in so many ways both big and small a life leading to this wonderful plateau. I recalled the first and only time I played in the NCAA Finals in 1966. This was the infamous game between Kentucky, my alma mater, and Texas Western. The first time in the history of the NCAA Championships that an all-white (Kentucky) starting five played against an all-black (Texas Western) starting five in the final game. It was also a time in America when tremendous civil unrest toward racism raised its ugly face. People rose up and fought against racist attitudes that divided this country. Texas Western (We Shall Overcome) won the game that day and captured the hearts, respect, and admiration of all American people, both black and white. That win reverberated through college athletics for years to come. Many schools in the South still practiced segregation and did not allow any black athletes to play. This game was a watershed event that led many great black players and people to stand up to racism and courageously enroll in many of these institutions. To this day, I am so proud of being part of that historical event, which played a part in great change. The highest form of sanity is change and when change raises its beautiful face, you adapt, you grow, you move on. America has moved on with this issue and we are better for it. Not long ago the Basketball Hall of Fame

honored Texas Western by inducting them into the Hall as a TEAM. Recently, a movie by Jerry Bruckheimer, appropriately titled *Glory Road,* immortalized this team in a moving, dynamic story chronicling their struggle to the top. It was a classic example embodying the tenets, beliefs, and passions of one of America's greatest leaders, Dr. Martin Luther King Jr. Yes. Texas Western HAD A DREAM and achieved it.

Texas Western won the 1966 NCAA Championship with an all-black starting five.

Chris and I talked about my junior year at Linton High School in Schenectady, New York, when I faced the great Lew Alcindor, a freshman center at Power Memorial. Even at that time, we all knew this graceful and incredibly gifted athlete was going to be very special. And he was, going to three of his own Final Fours with UCLA. I remembered my time at the University of Kentucky, learning the game under the watchful eye of Adolph Rupp, another Hall of Fame coach who got his start in basketball at the University of Kansas where the game's inventor, James Naismith, spent the latter part of his career. I incorporated much of Rupp's philosophy into my own teaching and, as if by fate, I eventually wound up the coach of the Los Angeles Lakers where I reconnected with Lew Alcindor, now Kareem Abdul-Jabbar, the once high school prodigy, always-cerebral person from New York. Needless to say, I liked having the sky hook in my corner better than trying to defend against the perfect offensive weapon. Kareem was the greatest player I ever coached. It was the combination of Kareem and Magic Johnson that started it all, leading me to the Hall of Fame. When Jerry West hired me to coach the Lakers in 1981, we had one of the great runs of any team **in NBA history.** That team won five championships in the 80s and is considered one of the greatest teams of all time. Those battles with the Sixers early, the Celtics in the mid-80s, and the epic Detroit bloodbaths against the great Chuck Daly-coached Piston "Bad Boys" teams in the late 80s, reset the direction of where the NBA was headed at the time. I believe that the 80s were the golden age of the NBA and

I was so proud to be part of it. **"A TEAM'S GREATEST FEAR WOULD BE ITS FEAR OF EXTINCTION, BUT, WHAT IT SHOULD FEAR EVEN MORE THAN THAT WOULD BE TO BECOME EXTINCT WITH INSIGNIFICANCE."** What that meant to me was that what you did as a team had to matter and count. What pride these teams had. The Lakers were the most SIGNIFICANT team of their time. If you were part of that team what you did mattered and counted. A TRUE CHAMPION THAT BECAME EXTINCT WITH SIGNIFICANCE.

As Chris and I continued our "talk" down memory lane, we gave pause to think about all of the influences in my life. Of course my parents, Lee and Mary Riley, gave me incredible support and confidence that I could be anything I wanted as long as I worked harder than others. The late, great Jim Valvano once said, and I parroted this message my whole life, is that "HARD WORK WON'T GUARANTEE YOU ANYTHING BUT WITHOUT IT YOU WON'T STAND A CHANCE." My parents instilled in me a work ethic and independence to succeed or fail on my own with great support either way and in doing so, they gave me everything. My father, unfortunately, left this world too early. I was only 25 and he missed what a dad would have liked to share – those successes and failures – with a son. His voice still rings strong in my mind from the time I ran home crying after getting beaten up in a game at the park. I was nine years old. I remember not wanting to go back. He told me that I was going back but that this experience would teach me not to be afraid of competition and that this would bring out the very best in me. I went back, competed and never ran again. As for my mom, she was there for many of my successes throughout life and enjoyed with my family all the joy and pain a life in playing and coaching this game brings. She was very familiar with the coaching life because my dad played and coached for many years in baseball. Yes, I was a proud son and brother of a family who always worked very hard and wanted to win. The DNA was there.

My high school coach, Walt Przybylo, caught me at that moment in life when I was stuck somewhere between being a boy and becoming a young man. HE TAUGHT ME THAT YOU HAD TO EARN IT IF YOU EVER GOT THE OPPORTUNITY. Needless to say, he gave me the push I needed and I am better for having known and played for him. These early influences eventually gave way to new figures in my life like Coach Adolph Rupp at Kentucky and later Jack McMahon, my first pro coach with the San Diego Rockets in 1967, who guided me as a young pro. Bill Sharman taught me the value of playing a distinctive and crucial role on the Laker team of 1972, the first team I won an NBA Championship with. My Laker teammate, friend, and later boss, Jerry West, along with Laker owner Jerry Buss, both believed I could coach and win. We did win, A LOT, and I thank them for their support. To Paul Westhead, who taught me the intricacies of practice planning, high-powered offenses, and the "box and none," THANK YOU.

Spending four years in New York with the Knicks would not have happened without Dave Checketts. We had a great run, almost winning the title in 94, but it was Hakeem Olajuwon, my fellow Hall of Fame teammate, who did us in. To all of the players I was blessed to have coached over the years who allowed me to get to this point – from Magic, Kareem, James Worthy, and so many others in L.A., to Patrick, Oak and John Starks in New York, to Zo, Tim, Shaq, DWade and many more in Miami: THANK YOU. To all the coaches who assisted me – Bill Bertka in LA, Dick Harter and Jeff Van Gundy in NY, Bob McAdoo, Stan Van Gundy, Keith Askins and Eric Spoelstra in Miami. AND SO MANY OTHERS: THANK YOU.

To Micky Arison, who provided me with the incredible platform in Miami to create and coach a team that I felt I could win with. He's the best owner in sports and whether it was good or bad, he let me figure it out. We won an NBA Championship in 2006 with this philosophy and after 14 years together we are still at it. Micky's encouragement and support is so appreciated. He knows I gave everything I had to give. The relationship we have formed and the experiences shared, will be FOREVER 15 STRONG.

However, the person I have received the most from, and who has endured the most while on this long journey to the Hall of Fame, is Christine Carolyn Rodstrom, better known as Chris Riley. SHE IS THE ONE. She kept it all together. My life, her life, and the lives of our two great children, James Patrick and Elisabeth

Marie, could not have been cultivated, nurtured or developed without Chris. She has not only supported me big-time, but inspired me to another level. This is a true partnership. When I was inducted into the Hall of Fame, they took both of us and if you ever read the Hall of Fame biography about me, you will read about Chris. If you ever look into the eyes of any of my pictures hanging in the Hall, you will see her sharp focus coming through. Whatever memorabilia you see hanging from the walls or placed in a glass box, she was behind it all. To get to this point YOU NEED SOMEONE unconditionally with you, come thick or thin. There are so many times when it may look like it will all break apart, all of it: the team, the game, the relationships, the families, and, at times, each other. This is a difficult road to navigate. Chris made sure that when we got to a fork in the road she knew which one to take. There is always fear. The fear you will lose something important and then you realize it's a forever life. "IN OUR DREAMS, OUR LOVE IS LOST … WE LIVE BY LUCK AND FATE … WE CARRY EACH OTHER INSIDE OF US AND PRAY THAT IT'S NOT TOO LATE … AND, AS WE STAND HERE ON THIS EMPTY ROAD WITH NOTHING AT OUR BACKS BUT THE WIND … DON'T WORRY BECAUSE WE ARE BACK IN EACH OTHER'S ARMS AGAIN." After 50 years of trying to be part of nothing but TEAMS, and after 40 years of being part of nothing but NBA TEAMS, and after 38 years of being part of nothing but the Chris and Pat TEAM, that's all I know. Getting to the Hall of Fame is being part

of this last great TEAM and being back in your arms again. Thank you, Chris.

I fell in love with basketball very early on and I am grateful the game has maintained its hold on me since the first time I picked up a ball. There is something beautiful in any game that requires a certain blend of power and finesse, speed and strength, size and intellect. The rhythm of the game and the nuances that make basketball so popular – jumping, passing, dribbling, shooting, running with abandon – compel even the most casual observer to take notice. And the entire human race seems to be paying attention as the game is played in every hamlet and small town, every city and neighborhood the world over. Basketball is reaching full maturity and for the last 50 years the Naismith Memorial Basketball Hall of Fame has been there to document the game's evolution from its birth in Springfield, Massachusetts, to the global phenomenon we see today. It has been an incredible honor and privilege to be part of it.

The next 50 years for the Basketball Hall of Fame promise to be even better. The new facility is world class, first rate in every possible way. The building itself is breathtaking and the stories that unfold as you wander through the gallery space grab you and pull you in as you serve as eyewitness to events that actually occurred decades ago. A collector myself, I stared in awe the first time I saw the jersey Wilt Chamberlain, a teammate of mine, wore the night he scored 100 points and I was also very proud to see so much memorabilia from the teams and players I was associated with over the years. The next generation of superstars will one day take their rightful place in the Hall of Fame, among the greatest ever. Guys like Alonzo Mourning, Shaquille O'Neal, and Dwayne Wade, who I coached in Miami, or Kobe Bryant, who redefines Showtime, or LeBron James, who proves basketball is still the ultimate team sport. And the Basketball Hall of Fame will still be there, celebrating the game and the traditions, the personalities, and the moments that make basketball America's new national pastime.

I remember like it was yesterday, those first words I said to a team the first game I coached in 1981, "YOU'RE EITHER WITH ME OR AGAINST ME. A HOUSE DIVIDED AGAINST ITSELF SURELY WILL NOT STAND." The Hall of Fame has stood hand in hand with all the great ones for 50 years as a team. The last words I said to a team the last game I coached in 2008, "A JOURNEY OF A THOUSAND MILES STARTS UNDER YOUR OWN TWO FEET, START WALKING." There are still so many more miles to go for all of those who one day will feel the honor to be part of this great Hall of Fame TEAM. Pat Riley ... Basketball Hall of Fame Class of 2008 and proud of it. You're either in or out. I am IN.

Thank You, Dave

The Naismith Memorial Basketball Hall of Fame dedicates this book to David R. "Dave" Gavitt in appreciation of his tremendous leadership as Hall of Fame Board Chairman from 1995 to 2004. His love of the game and respect for its history was the guiding force behind our magnificent new Hall of Fame.

INTRODUCTION

Since 1959, the Naismith Memorial Basketball Hall of Fame has honored and celebrated the game's greatest moments and brightest stars. On the occasion of its 50th Anniversary, we look back as the greatest shrine to the greatest game fulfills its steadfast promise to be the world's finest sports museum.

It began humbly.

The first manifestation of the Basketball Hall of Fame occupied a small piece of real estate on the campus of Springfield (MA) College, just a midrange jump shot from where the game was first played on December 21, 1891. That day, a physical education instructor named James Naismith introduced a new game to his class of 18 young men in an otherwise unremarkable gymnasium at the YMCA International Training School in Springfield.

The objective of this new game seemed simple enough: throw a round ball into a round basket tacked to a balcony 10 feet above the floor. But the winning team in that first game managed only one basket, on a 25-foot toss by William Chase. The pace of the game was slow and its origins humble, but the new pastime spread quickly, and by 1894, basketball was already being played in France, China, India, and more than a dozen other nations.

The original Basketball Hall of Fame opened its doors to the public on February 17, 1968, during a pivotal time for the sport. Just a month before, on January 20, 1968, Elvin Hayes had just led the University of Houston to a thrilling 71-69 victory over Lew Alcindor and the Bruins of UCLA in college basketball's version of the Game of the Century. More than 50,000 fans packed the Houston Astrodome that night and millions more watched from home as this epic battle was the first-ever regular season game to be broadcast live on national television.

Only three days after that watershed moment, New York's Madison Square Garden played host to the 18th annual NBA All-Star Game. The star-studded lineups included future Hall of Famers Oscar Robertson and Jerry Lucas, Elgin Baylor and Jerry West, Wilt Chamberlain and Willis Reed, not to mention Boston's own triple threat of Bill Russell, John Havlicek, and Sam Jones. For the first time in its history,

The original Basketball Hall of Fame opened its doors to the public on February 17, 1968.

basketball was front and center in the minds of sports fans across the country.

The grand opening of the Hall in 1968, while timely, was actually the culmination of a game plan that had begun more than 30 years before.

The seeds were planted in 1936 when the United States defeated Canada 19-8 in the gold medal game of the Berlin Olympics. Dr. Naismith, a Canadian himself, attended the game thanks to the generosity and foresight of the National Association of Basketball Coaches, which raised enough money in the months leading up to the Opening Ceremony to send the game's inventor, all expenses paid, to Berlin. Naismith later called this his proudest moment and the sight of his game being played on the international stage stirred his emotions.

Before long the NABC took up an even greater cause – a capital campaign to erect a memorial to the late Dr. Naismith and his wonderful game. America's entry into World War II on December 8, 1941, postponed any thoughts of a

Hall of Fame, but in 1949 the NABC renewed its commitment to honor the game and its inventor. Ten years later, in 1959, despite the absence of a physical structure to call home, the Basketball Hall of Fame was incorporated and its first class of inductees was announced.

The Hall of Fame experienced some growing pains during its first two decades on the campus of Springfield College. Each year, several thousand visitors flocked to the birthplace of basketball to be inspired by the stories and memorabilia on display. The Hall had outgrown its original confines.

Aware of the need for the Hall's expansion, efforts were underway to make the Hall of Fame the world's premier source of basketball information. In 1979, with the cooperation and support of a local organizing committee, the Basketball Hall of Fame sponsored the inaugural Tip-Off Classic, an early season game that signaled the official start of the college basketball season. The Tip-Off Classic pitted the nation's top teams against one another, and in its 27 years, featured such storied programs as Kentucky, Duke, North Carolina, UCLA, Indiana, and Kansas.

One of the "hallowed halls" within the original Naismith basketball shrine.

In the early 1980s, the popularity of the game soared to unprecedented heights and the Basketball Hall of Fame was poised to take flight. The rivalry between Larry Bird and Magic Johnson, which first set the nets on fire at the 1979 NCAA Final Four, breathed new life into Dr. Naismith's game. Bird versus Magic struck a chord with basketball fans everywhere and NBA action was, as its advertising campaign promised, fantastic.

June 30, 1985, marked the grand opening of a brand-new Hall of Fame.

Meanwhile, at the University of North Carolina, another kind of bird was about to spread his wings. Flight 23 was cleared for takeoff, tongue wagging from somewhere high above the clouds, hanging in mid-air, and finally returning to earth to change the game forever. His name? Why, Michael Jordan, of course.

As Bird, Magic, Michael and many others pushed the popularity of basketball to a fever pitch in the early 1980s, basketball was about to turn 100 years old and the need for a more appropriate shrine to reflect the game's growth and development was clear.

On June 30, 1985, more than 10,000 basketball fans descended upon the city of Springfield, including weatherman Willard Scott of NBC's *The Today Show*, for the dedication and grand opening of a brand-new Hall of Fame. Three levels of basketball history welcomed visitors that day and new high-tech exhibits gave the museum a futuristic look and feel. The Spalding Shootout, an interactive phenomenon where visitors of all ages shot hoops from a moving platform, proved most popular that first day and remained so every day thereafter. The sprawling new museum, with its fast-paced activity and cutting-edge technology, attracted visitors from every state in the Union and six of the seven continents.

Also in 1985, the Basketball Hall of Fame entered a new era by being the first to recognize the contributions women have made to the game. Senda Berenson Abbott, the First Lady of Basketball, introduced the new game to the women of Smith College in 1892, just a few months after its invention. Bertha Teague coached at Byng High School in Ada, Oklahoma, for 42 straight seasons, winning eight state championships. Margaret Wade patrolled the sidelines at Delta State University, and though her time there was short, she captured three consecutive AIAW national championships from 1975 to 1977. The

Basketball Hall of Fame was becoming more inclusive, a reflection of the game itself.

The 1985 version of the Basketball Hall of Fame witnessed its share of historic milestones and championship moments. Basketball celebrated its 100th birthday in grand style on December 21, 1991, by returning to its place of birth for a centennial gala. More than a dozen basketball luminaries helped blow out the candles that day, including the good doctor Julius Erving, the bespectacled George Mikan, the great amateur Bob Kurland, the irrepressible Rick Barry, and the famed coach John McLendon. Duke's Mike Krzyzewski became the first coach since John Wooden to win back-to-back NCAA national championships in 1992, the same year the United States Dream Team captured gold at the summer Olympics. In 1997 the WNBA, a women's professional league, exploded onto the American sports scene.

Once again, the tremendous growth and popularity of the game forced a second relocation and in 2000 construction began on the third Hall of Fame.

In September of 2002, on the occasion of the new building's spectacular grand opening celebration, the Hall welcomed Coaches Larry Brown, Lute Olson, and Kay Yow, and players Drazen Petrovic and Magic Johnson as the first Inductees to take their rightful place in the new Honors Ring. The Honors Ring overlooks Center Court, an iconic, breathtaking, full-size regulation basketball court where the game never ends. On any given day, visitors lace 'em

The Hall of Fame is home to nearly 300 basketball immortals.

up to play under the basketball heavens, reliving the glory days of yesteryear or practicing for the big games yet to come.

Today, the Naismith Memorial Basketball Hall of Fame is home to nearly 300 inductees and more than 40,000 square feet of basketball history. Located on the picturesque banks of the Connecticut River, the new museum is a fitting shrine to the game Dr. Naismith invented more than a century ago. The landmark structure is one of the world's most distinctive monuments punctuating the Springfield skyline and stirring the spirits of basketball fans everywhere. Hundreds of interactive exhibits share the spotlight with skills challenges, live clinics, and shooting contests. And, of course, there is enough basketball history to impress the world's most avid sports fans!

After decades of growth, the Naismith Memorial Basketball Hall of Fame celebrates its 50th Anniversary in 2009. It has evolved from its humble origins to become Hoops Heaven … the earthly home of the game's immortals.

The Hall of Fame stirs the spirits of fans everywhere.

THE CLASS OF 2009

On its 50th Anniversary, the

Naismith Memorial Hall of Fame

inducts one of its best classes

ever. Joining the game's greats

in 2009:

Michael Jordan

David Robinson

Jerry Sloan

John Stockton

and

C. Vivian Stringer

The Class of 2009: Greatest of all time?

By Jim Krause

A Golden Anniversary – a celebration of 50 years – is always special. And in 2009, the Naismith Memorial Basketball Hall of Fame is having a Golden Anniversary to remember.

The Hall of Fame inducts its 50th anniversary class in September of 2009. This class takes its place in history with the previous 49 because of what the five individuals in the class have accomplished in their careers, and also because of their continued fame in the sport today. In the case of each of the five inductees, they did things that continue to represent standards for excellence.

Two of the five inductees are known more for their leadership on the sidelines than for their accomplishments on the court. **C. Vivian Stringer,** currently the head women's basketball coach at Rutgers University, set the bar for all women who enter the realm of coaching and she

C. Vivian Stringer is the only coach to take three college programs to the NCAA Final Four.

did so at a time when African-Americans faced discrimination and all women battled exclusion.

Jerry Sloan, the coach of the NBA's Utah Jazz, set coaching standards for winning, but even more proudly set standards for loyalty. At a time when it was not in vogue to ride out bad times, to build and re-build teams, and to stand by owners and players, Sloan did just that.

The other three inductees were all-time great players: **John Stockton, David Robinson, and Michael Jordan**. We'll tell their stories later.

But first …

Stringer began her coaching career at a time when African-Americans were not accepted in main-stream athletic programs. During this same era, support for women's programs came at a great expense to the coach and to college administrations. Title IX was a vague statute virtually ignored by the leaders of institutions of higher learning and it would be years later, after Stringer had already made a mark in women's basketball, that some support for women's sports would come. If historians accurately report her influence, they will mention her in the same breath with John McLendon, Ben Jobe and John Thompson when discussing coaches who had a great impact in eliminating discrimination in basketball.

Stringer is the only coach to take three college programs to the NCAA Final Four. The first trip came in 1982, when she led Cheney State College of Pennsylvania to the very first NCAA Women's Final Four. No one paid much attention to the historically black college and what a job it had taken to gain the respect of administrators, coaches, officials and fans. The Lady Wolves lost in the finals to Louisiana Tech University.

Iowa was the second coaching stop for Stringer and she took the Lady Hawkeyes to the Final Four in 1993. She would later continue her astonishing run of success with Rutgers University, which made NCAA Final Four appearances in 2000 and 2007.

Stringer had a number of opportunities working with young women in international competitions and was a member of the staff when the USA won the Olympic Gold Medal in 2004. She was identified as one of the "101 Most Influential Minorities in Sport" by *Sports Illustrated* in 2003.

Clearly, **C. Vivian Stringer** is an influential person, an inspirational person, and a pioneer in the sport of basketball.

"The Original Bull" was a reference to **Jerry Sloan** being selected first by the NBA expansion franchise Bulls in Chicago, but it also applies to his approach to coaching. As a player, Sloan was an effective scorer, and he even earned some All-American honors in college for his scoring efficiency. But in the NBA, he gained a reputation as a tenacious defender.

His leadership and dedication to stopping the

Did You Know?

For the **1990-91** NCAA men's season, two free throws are awarded with a team's 10th personal foul of the half, and three free throws are given to a player fouled beyond the three-point arc while shooting.

Beginning with the **1993-94** season, the college men's shot clock is reduced to 35 seconds; the clock stops after each basket during the final minute.

Jerry Sloan is known as the "Original Bull."

opposition was recognized around the NBA as he garnered All-Defensive First-Team honors four times.

Injuries ended Sloan's playing career in 1976, but he remained in the NBA as a scout and an assistant coach. His first attempt as a head coach was less than successful when he took over the Chicago Bulls in 1979 and suffered through a record of 94-121 during a three-year span. During a brief exile back to the ranks of scouting, and some coaching in the Continental Basketball Association, Sloan returned as an assistant with the Utah Jazz in 1984 and in 1988 was named Utah's head coach.

Sloan will forever be linked with Jazz players John Stockton and Karl Malone. The dynamic pair of NBA All-Stars epitomized Sloan's hard-nosed style and commitment to defense and team play. It was the toughness needed to succeed in the NBA that Sloan exhibited in his playing career and imparted to his players on the Jazz. This attitude played a huge role in the yearly success enjoyed by the franchise. While Stockton was known for his league-leading assist numbers, he also was named to the NBA All-Defensive Team five times, an echo of Sloan's days with the Chicago Bulls.

With the end of the 2009 season, Jerry Sloan had won more than 1,100 games in the NBA and had led the Jazz to the playoffs 16 consecutive years. Utah has enjoyed 11 seasons with more than 50 wins and has won the NBA Western Conference six times. Twice, Utah has earned a spot in the NBA finals, losing both times to Michael Jordan and the Chicago Bulls.

With all of these accomplishments, Sloan has set himself apart from other coaches in the NBA by setting records for wins and years on the bench with a single franchise. During the 2008-2009 season, he won game number 1,000 as the head coach of the Jazz and with a new contract in hand for 2009-2010, the record will continue to grow. In the present coaching environment, where moving on to the next challenge is prevalent, he remains an example of the loyal servant.

Throughout Sloan's coaching career, he has been destined to hoist the second-place trophy. He lost in his only two Finals and finished second a few times in the NBA Coach of the Year balloting. But with his induction into the Naismith Memorial Basketball Hall of Fame, Sloan takes his rightful place among the game's greats.

It will be argued that the 2009 Naismith Memorial Basketball Hall of Fame induction class is the greatest of all time. Older fans might argue that the 1980 class that included Jerry Lucas, Oscar Robertson and Jerry West was an equal representation of greatness, but there is no comparison to the body of work that has been achieved by **David Robinson, John Stockton** and **Michael Jordan**. The broad scope of championships, gold medals and individual awards from college and professional basketball simply has no comparison. When you add the elite standards that these three great competitors set for those who follow, the decision must be unanimous.

Stockton set the standard for commitment to team by setting NBA records in both assists and steals. David Robinson parlayed his wonderful preparation in the United States Navy into an incredible NBA career. And Michael Jordan

John Stockton recorded nearly 16,000 assists in his NBA career.

became a legend and a brand name synonymous with basketball.

Each was selected as one of the 50 Greatest Players in basketball history. They each won Olympic Gold Medals, hold scores of individual achievements, and most interestingly, were cited numerous times for their defensive skills during an era when the NBA was promoting scoring and the offensive talents of its stars.

John Stockton played point guard. There were many who played the position before him, including Bob Cousy and Magic Johnson, who were deemed the greatest at that position. But when Stockton came on the scene, he redefined the position and rewrote the record book, setting standards that future NBA players will be hard-pressed to match.

Stockton was selected 16th in the first round of the NBA draft in 1984 following an excellent collegiate career at Gonzaga University. After averaging more than 20 points a game in college, he expanded his game to meet the needs of the talent accumulated by the Utah Jazz and completed his professional career averaging a double-double (13.5 points and 10.5 assists). At the conclusion of his 19-year NBA career, Stockton had recorded 15,806 assists, an NBA record that far exceeds second place. He also owns the assist record for five of the top six

individual seasons ever in the NBA. Stockton also set the NBA standard for steals in a career with 3,265, maybe the only time that someone pushed Michael Jordan to second place.

Like Sloan, his coach in Utah, Stockton set standards of loyalty with additional NBA records: seasons with the same team and consecutive games played with the same team.

Although his quiet demeanor and reluctance to use his fame for financial gain probably cost him some cash, he was never overlooked by his peers or basketball fans when it came to recognition. Stockton provided the modern model for point guard play, and his willingness to provide opportunities for his teammates and his franchise will be a legacy hard to match.

The greatest basketball player ever to come out of a service academy? That sort of designation usually takes some good fortune, and in the case of **David Robinson**, that is exactly what happened.

When he entered the Naval Academy at Annapolis, Maryland, Robinson signed in at 6'6" tall. He was well under the maximum height allowed by the academy and diligently applied himself to his studies and his sports activities. Upon leaving Annapolis, the "Admiral" was a solid 7-footer, then exceeding the height limits, and exceeding

Did You Know?

The NCAA changes the intentional foul rule to two shots plus possession of the ball in men's basketball for the **1987-88** season, and for women's games the following season.

1992: The NBA shortens its three-point line to a uniform 22 feet from the basket.

1997: The NBA three-point line is lengthened to its original distance of 23'9" (except in the corners, where it remains at 22 feet).

David Robinson won one MVP award in his NBA career.

the expectations of Navy basketball. He became a national sensation and was drafted in the first round in 1987 by the San Antonio Spurs.

The Spurs understood that Robinson had a multi-year military obligation and therefore might not be available to play for them immediately, but they could not pass on "the next great big man." Two years into a five-year military requirement, Robinson was allowed to forgo the remaining years and begin leading the Spurs to the pinnacle of the NBA.

Like many of his peers, he has enough individual awards to clutter a personal library, but he also led the Spurs to two NBA championships. What separates Robinson from many is the breadth of his NBA skills. Along with being Rookie of the Year in 1990, he received awards for scoring, defense, rebounding, sportsmanship, blocked shots, and community service. He was so powerful in community service that the NBA eventually named its annual service award after Robinson. He won one league MVP award and was named one of the 50 Greatest Players. He also was selected to play on three United States Olympic basketball teams.

But his unique accolade is this: Robinson is the only player in NBA history to win the league awards for blocked shots, rebounding, and scoring while also being named Rookie of the Year, Defensive Player of the Year and NBA MVP. Additionally, he is the only NBA player who ended a season with averages in scoring, rebounding, blocked shots and steals that all were among the top five. That is why he is different from all the rest.

Robinson became known for his philanthropy when he challenged a group of San Antonio youngsters to remain in school. He pledged to give them money toward college if they did so. In 1998, he gave $8,000 to each student who met that challenge. Also, he and his wife, Valerie, created the Carver Academy in San Antonio and continue to support the school with contributions in the millions of dollars.

Robinson continues to represent his family, the U.S. Navy, the NBA, and the game of basketball in a manner that qualifies him to join the other greats honored in the Naismith Memorial Basketball Hall of Fame.

The challenge to briefly and accurately describe why **Michael Jordan** is the greatest player of all time is a very daunting task. Where does one begin?

With helping Hall of Fame coach Dean Smith to win his first of two NCAA National Championships at North Carolina?

With Jordan's three consecutive NBA championships with the Chicago Bulls, followed by a few years of trying to make it in major league baseball, and then a second three-peat in the NBA?

One could list the five MVP awards, the 14 All-Star appearances, the Defensive Player of the Year or even a Rookie of the Year award, but even that would be an incomplete accounting of his greatness.

Jordan matched Robinson, winning the two most coveted awards in college basketball: the Naismith and Wooden trophies. He even received an ESPY award as the "Athlete of the Century."

Michael Jordan won five MVP awards in his NBA career.

Jordan is easily identified as the greatest No. 3 pick in the history of the NBA Draft. Can you imagine that two NBA teams actually selected other players before him?

He had a profound impact on basketball world-wide. He introduced basketball to the rest of the world. International teams played a version of the game, but they did not play it like Mike. His shoes and his jerseys became fashion staples, and not just kids in North Carolina or even in the United States wanted to be like Mike – the world wanted to be like Mike. What is astonishing today, years after his third retirement in 2003, is that his legacy is alive and his brand is as strong as ever.

If you polled kids around the world and showed them the logo of the NBA, how many could tell you that the player in the logo was Jerry West? How many of those same kids would recognize the Jordan logo with him dunking the ball with his arms extended and his legs flared out? Chris Broussard of *ESPN The Magazine* compared Jordan's six championships to the one championship won by Jerry West. West played at times with Wilt Chamberlain and Elgin Baylor, both Hall of Famers, and won one championship in seven tries in the NBA Finals and he was nicknamed "Mr. Clutch." Jordan played with Scottie Pippen and Dennis Rodman and won six NBA championships. "Athlete of the Century" is definitely the appropriate nickname for Jordan.

What will be his legacy … as a player? As a person? As an icon of the game?

Steve Schanwald, Executive Vice President-Business Operations for the Bulls, said:

"In my view, Michael was the first athlete to come along (even including great ones like Ruth, DiMaggio, Ali, Gretzky, etc.), who was a perfect 10 at all aspects, on and off the court, of what we hope for in our professional athletes.

"He was a 10 offensively. He played with a real joy. He practiced as hard as he played. He was a 10 defensively. He was a 10 athletically. He was a 10 in his basketball IQ. He was a 10 when it came to dealing with the media. He was a 10 in terms of how he dressed in public. He was a 10 in terms of how he packaged and marketed himself and in how he built his brand and carefully nurtured his image. There was never any hint of scandal. And he did all this at a time when basketball was exploding around the world in Europe, South America, and Asia, and when new and traditional forms of media (satellite and cable TV and the Internet) were making the world a smaller place.

"Whatever 'it' is, he had 'it.' There was just such a presence about him. His charisma was and remains second to none."

The Naismith Memorial Basketball Hall of Fame will find it challenging to match the Class of 2009 in years ahead. Attempting to do just that will ensure the selection process is diligent and that future generations will enjoy those who have truly separated themselves in the world of basketball.

Jordan rises to greatness.

Robinson (left) exceeded expectations.
Sloan (above) represents hard work.

Congratulations to the Class of 2009

The iconic MJ.

Stockton was "pass-first."

Stringer opened doors for women.

BEGINNINGS

BEGINNINGS

From Dr. James Naismith's invention of the game to the founding of the ABA, "Beginnings" represent the important "firsts" in the history of basketball.

The Origins of Basketball

By Jim O'Connell

Few have fulfilled an assignment the way Dr. James Naismith did.

Imagine, complying with a request from your boss and having it impact millions of lives over 100-plus years and with no end in sight to its effectiveness.

Phrases like ``well done'' or ``thank you'' seem so inadequate in trying to grasp what happened in Springfield, Massachusetts, in December 1891.

James Naismith was born in Ontario, Canada, on November 6, 1861, and had a rough, rural early life as he, his brother and his sister were orphaned in 1870 when their parents died after contracting typhoid fever.

Growing up under the care of relatives, Naismith was an accomplished athlete, playing hockey on

No dunks, no slams, no jams ... long before we envisioned the high-flying game we know today, basketball began with a simple peach basket.

skates he made for himself. He spent considerable time farming, logging and handling the chores of the time that so many children did. He never let his studies lag and, despite taking time away from school to help his family, he graduated from high school in 1883 and headed for McGill University in Montreal.

Naismith earned a bachelor's degree in physical education, participating in rugby, lacrosse and gymnastics, and establishing his background for the impact he would soon have on the world.

He entered the Presbyterian College of Theology in Montreal after graduation from McGill, and while working as an instructor in McGill's physical education program, completed his stud-

ies at Presbyterian in three years, establishing the lifestyle of a man who would serve so many in a long life devoted to others.

His combination of studies in theology and physical education led him to the Young Men's Christian Association, which had made its way from Europe decades before. The YMCA training school was located in Springfield, Massachusetts, and it was there that Naismith focused his future through spiritual and physical development, his and others.

Sports were becoming a big part of collegiate life. Track and field, football and baseball, fledgling sports themselves, and rugby were the most popular in the Eastern part of the United

Headline writers used to refer to players as "cagers" because early games literally were played in cages like this one.

States, but they were all sports meant to be played outdoors and weather was restricting what the athletes could do in the winter months.

Dr. Luther Halsey Gulick was the director of the physical education department at Springfield College and was the man Naismith reported to as an instructor there.

Gulick, as part of a seminar in psychology he taught, decided there was a need to create an interesting indoor game that could give the athletes who had put away their football pads and were waiting to start using their baseball gloves something to do during the winter besides running laps in a gym.

Naismith had two major objectives as he worked on Gulick's request. He wanted to "make it fair for all players, and free of rough play."

The balls being used in the sports of the day ranged from the larger ones used for rugby and football to the much smaller baseball. Naismith decided on using the soccer ball because it would be easier to throw in a confined area. To reduce the temptation of tackling or making contact with the person with the ball, he decided there would be no running with the ball.

To eliminate having to get through others to cross a goal line in order to score, Naismith decided to put the goal over the players' heads, by far the most dramatic decision about the new sport. The height of 10 feet came about because that was how high the railing at the gymnasium was. A peach basket was hung for the players to try to reach, and a ladder was next to each basket with a person assigned to remove the ball from it after each score.

Naismith simplified his game with 13 rules. The current rule books may be a lot more detailed and intricate and cover almost every possibility imaginable, but Naismith's original 13 rules did an amazing job of putting together an activity that com- bined vigorous exercise with the chance for competition.

An early basket came equipped with a pull-chain to release the ball from the basket.

A look at the original 13 rules almost 120 years later is staggering. All or part of eight of the rules are still in effect. Imagine, 120 years later the time allotted for inbounding the ball is still five seconds. Goaltending is still illegal. You can still hear players yell "walking" when an opponent takes an extra step.

On December 21, 1891, the new game made its debut. Within a few days the reviews were very positive. A new sport - basket ball - had been born. The dreary winter days suddenly had something that appealed to athletes.

The next year, the magazine *Triangle* had an article about it titled "A New Game."

Here is where Naismith's humility helped form the future lexicon of the sport. A gentleman named Frank Mahan demanded the new sport be called "Naismith Ball." Thankfully, Naismith declined.

The game became known simply as basketball. A title that describes so much of what the game is about as well as one that fit perfectly into the American landscape.

Naismith and Gulick published the rules in 1894 in the "American Sports Publishing Company" and the game was now being played outside New England.

Naismith left the next year for Denver where he was the physical education director at the YMCA and also attended the University of Colorado Medical School, graduating in 1898.

That year he moved his family again, this time to the University of Kansas where he became director of the gymnasium, campus chaplain, and basketball coach. He coached his sport at Kansas for eight years, but stayed in Lawrence, teaching at his adopted school, for the rest of his life. He became an American citizen in 1925.

In 1929, G.L. Pierce received a U.S. patent for the basketball we know today. Naismith's gift to the world was complete with the addition of iron hoops, nets and court dimensions over the years.

The rest of Naismith's life involved so much more than basketball. He served two separate stints in World War I, published two books—*A Modern College* and *Essence of a Healthy Life*—worked again for the YMCA, this time on an international level, received doctorates from the two colleges he attended and was made a Professor Emeritus at Kansas.

Barney Sedran starred on pro teams from 1911-1926.

In 1936, just 45 years after Naismith completed his assignment by inventing a sport, basketball was added to the Olympics. Enough countries—many because American soldiers and sailors were able to play it wherever they were deployed around the world—had accepted basketball that it became an Olympic sport.

Naismith was unable to afford the expense of getting to Berlin, Germany, for the debut of his sport in the Olympics. The National Association of Basketball Coaches created the "Naismith Fund," and donations from its membership, current and former players and people who had simply become fans of the sport allowed Naismith to be there on April 7, 1936, when he tossed the ceremonial ball for the first Olympic basketball match. He was quoted often that that day was the highlight of his life.

Dr. James Naismith died on November 29, 1939.

His was a life so full. An educator, a physician, an instructor, a spiritual leader, an author, a husband, and a father. All those titles would be enough to make any man's time among us full and deserving of thanks.

Naismith had one more title bestowed on him: inventor.

His wintertime diversion that started with nine players on each side and a peach basket at both ends of a gymnasium, became as big a part of Americana as any other sport, game or recreational activity.

He got to see his sport on the collegiate level and in the Olympics, but there was still so much to come. March Madness and the NBA became the landscape for basketball in the United States.

Those original countries that participated in the Olympics were joined by others on six continents and basketball's growth is still unlimited worldwide.

Naismith gave us a game that can be played with five on each team in an organized situation or with any number on a side anywhere a hoop can be hung. It is an exercise that can even be enjoyed practicing alone, in a gym, a park or a driveway. It is something that brings the joy of a successful shot or pass and the frustration of a miss or mistake.

James Naismith (left) didn't think basketball should be coached; Phog Allen thought otherwise.

In 1959, he was inducted into basketball's Hall of Fame, a building that now bears his name.

Almost 12 decades after he fulfilled an assignment that went on to impact millions of lives, it is only right to say "well done" and "thank you" to Dr. James Naismith.

You Can't Coach Basketball, You Just Play It

By Blair Kerkhoff

Talk about a visionary.

Phog Allen wanted to coach basketball before most understood the concept.

At the beginning of the 20th century, college basketball teams had managers. They had captains. Kansas even had the game's inventor, Dr. James Naismith, accompany its team.

But Naismith didn't consider himself a coach, and few at the time thought of basketball as an activity that needed instruction, promotion or motivation.

Allen did, and the story of his transition from a young player to a coach became a staple on the lecture circuit during his retirement. He recalled the day Naismith called him into his office.

"I've got a good joke on you, you bloody beggar. They want you to coach basketball down at Baker," Allen recalled Naismith's message.

"What's so funny about that?" Allen said.

"Why, you can't coach basketball—you just play it," Naismith is to have said.

Pause for laughter.

"Well, you certainly can coach free-throw shooting," Allen was to have replied. "And you can teach the boys to pass at angles and run in curves. You can show them how to arc their shots, and pivot to the sideline instead of into the court where a guard can get the ball."

Dramatic pause.

"I don't think it changed his mind," Allen would continue. "But I thought a coach was necessary if the game was going to grow. By this token, you can see how many basketball coaches today are making money under false pretenses."

More laughter.

Whether the conversation or something like it took place only Allen and Naismith knew for sure, and after the inventor's death in 1939, some 17 seasons before Allen's forced retirement at Kansas, the inventor was no longer around to refute it.

But it made for a good story.

Allen wasn't basketball's first coach, although he was among the first to become a paid coach. He wasn't Kansas' first coach or college basketball's first great coach.

But he was the first whose career was considered legendary, and from no less a figure than Naismith came the title Allen deserves. A framed picture of Naismith to Allen was inscribed "From the father of basketball to the father of basketball coaching."

A coaching career that included 746 victories— the most in college basketball when he left the game in 1956—an NCAA championship, two other teams designated as national champions by the Helms Foundation, an Olympic gold medal, 24 conference championships and the successful recruitment of such luminaries as Wilt Chamberlain and Clyde Lovellette is only part of Allen's story.

Perhaps nobody contributed more to basketball than Allen. He was the founding president of the National Association of Basketball Coaches. He did more than anybody to have basketball added to the Olympics. He helped rescue the NCAA Tournament from financial ruin.

Phog Allen was the first to insist that basketball could be coached.

Allen helped start the Kansas Relays, the famous track and field meet; build the school's football stadium, and once staged the world championship of basketball, at least for that month.

Allen realized before anyone else that the most valuable member of a team was one who knew how to treat injuries, and he took it upon himself to be that person. He was a trained osteopath and treated his players, opposing players and athletes in other sports. It's why he was known throughout his career as "Doc" Allen.

Allen was committed to developing fundamentals. His teams would spend the first couple of weeks of every season working on two-handed chest and hook passes. As for shooting, Allen preferred the bank shot, with the shooter's thumbs placed on the sides of the ball.

He created carom shot lanes for practice drills. Allen would dress in sweats and demonstrate every drill.

He liked his offense patterned with set plays from the point guard, whom Allen called his "center" because he was the center of the offense.

Always looking at ways to improve the game, Allen often found himself leading discussions on rules changes. When the great Doc Meanwell wanted to eliminate the dribble in 1927, Allen led the charge to block the movement.

But a rule change Allen championed throughout his career was never enacted. As early as the 1920s, Allen thought baskets should be 12 feet high instead of 10.

He preferred the higher hoop for several reasons. By Allen's calculations—and he kept a notebook full of this data—80 percent of the fouls occurred around the basket as smaller players attempted to prevent larger ones from catching the ball or scoring easy hoops. And until 1944, four fouls meant disqualification.

Allen hated the tip-in, believing it rewarded an offense for missing a shot, and he abhorred the dunk, which was legal although not possible for many players in the pre-World War II days. Allen called tall players "mezzanine peeping toms" or "goons."

But on a 12-foot basket, Allen reasoned the action would move away from the basket and relieve the congestion. It would eliminate goal-tending by the defense, which was legal until 1944, and remove the "goalie" from basketball. The three-second lane would no longer be necessary because taller players wouldn't stand under the basket. Also, with a 12-foot goal, Allen believed field goals should be worth three points.

So convinced that basketball would eventually see things his way, Allen kept a pair of 12-foot goals at the practice floor in Robinson Hall on the campus at the University of Kansas. In 1934, the Jayhawks actually played two games against rival Kansas State with 12-foot goals that counted on the overall record. The Wildcats won the first one, Kansas the second. Field goals counted three points.

Ironically, as much as he tried to reduce the influence of the big man throughout his career, Allen didn't win an NCAA Tournament until he recruited the giant Lovellette from Terre Haute, Indiana.

But above all, and more meaningful to him than anything else, Allen was a coach.

He liked coaching so much that his career started by coaching two different teams for three straight years.

Allen coached while he was playing, a typical arrangement in those days, except Allen was playing for one school and coaching another.

In the fall of 1905, just before the beginning of Allen's freshman and only year at Kansas, he met with a delegation from Baker, a small college near Lawrence. He agreed to become the team's basketball coach.

It was quite a busy school year for Allen in 1905-06. For the first time, Kansas had agreed to abide by the eligibility rules of the conference that would become known as the Big Ten. Freshmen were ineligible for the first semester. So Allen and another standout named Tommy Johnson formed the nucleus of the school's first freshmen team. They beat the varsity in one of three games that winter.

Allen made his varsity debut on Feb. 8, 1906, and his first start came four days later against Nebraska. Allen scored 23 points in his first game, a 37-17 victory. In his final game that season, he scored a school-record 26 in an easy triumph over Emporia.

The Jayhawks finished 12-7 and it was the school's best basketball record to date.

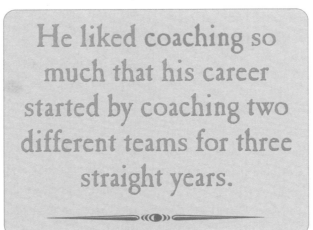

He liked coaching so much that his career started by coaching two different teams for three straight years.

When Kansas wasn't playing, Allen made his way to Baker. Both of Allen's teams were scheduled to meet late in the season but the game was called off when Allen came up with a hand injury and couldn't play.

Allen's future as a college athlete looked bright. But when his Baker team went 18-3, Allen was more satisfied with his sideline success. Plus, he needed to pay the bills.

Living expenses in Lawrence were too great. Baker offered room, board and a small stipend.

A coaching career that would last a half-century had started, and Allen's next stop took him to high school. Independence, Missouri, where Allen attended, had started football the previous year and he became the team's second coach, in 1907. He also coached the school's basketball team that year.

His second team at Baker finished 14-0, which included a triumph over Kansas. Allen would have been a sophomore star for those Jayhawks. Instead, the team that would be the last with Naismith listed as the head coach, finished 7-8, and it made Allen officially 1-0 against the game's inventor who believed his game was never meant to be coached.

"The great difficulties in developing a team are the lack of suitable quarterbacks in which to train and the lack of a coach," the school paper reported. "Dr. James Naismith, the inventor of the game, is so busy with his work as athletic director that he rarely finds time to give the men thorough training."

Naismith took care of both problems when the 1907 season ended. He resigned as basketball coach and oversaw completion of a new gym.

Kansas needed a new coach, and basketball was growing more popular with the news the school was joining Missouri, Nebraska, Iowa and Washington University of St. Louis in forming the Missouri Valley Conference. The 1907-08 schedule included six games against conference members playing for a trophy.

Who else but Allen would become the coach?

In what could have been his junior year, the 22-year-old Allen became the first person paid to coach basketball at Kansas, and basketball advanced to another level of importance on campus.

The Jayhawks played their most ambitious schedule in 1907-08 and their 18-6 record was the best to date. That season, Kansas won all six games against Missouri Valley opponents to become the first conference champion.

The next year would be even better. The Jayhawks won their first 19 games and finished with a 25-3 record. The victory total would stand as a school mark until the 1952 NCAA championship team won 28 games.

Allen had stopped coaching Baker in 1908-09, but he did coach Haskell, the Indian school in Lawrence, and led that team to a 27-5 record, including 19 victories during a 24-game road tour.

In one basketball season, Allen's teams went 52-8, although throughout his life his records at schools besides Kansas were listed inaccurately, probably because historians relied on Allen's memory for the numbers.

Good train service was said to have allowed Allen to coach three teams in one year: Kansas, Baker and Haskell. But research proved it never happened and Allen's records were adjusted in 1990.

Now came another important pivot point in Allen's career. He left Kansas after the 1909 season to enter the Central College of Osteopathy in Kansas City, and in 1912, began a second phase of his coaching career, at the

Gymnasium in the School for Christian Workers, where the first Basketball Scrimmage took place December 1891. Armory Hill Y.M.C.A also used these facilities 1885 to 1894.

school today known as the University of Central Missouri in Warrensburg.

He never lived a dull moment at Central Missouri, once getting his school kicked out of the conference when allegations of cheating surfaced. Once, an opponent accused him of poisoning the drinking water and creating a diarrhea epidemic.

Allen coached baseball and football as well as basketball, and he walked off the field of his first football game a 127-0 winner over the Kemper Military Academy.

Always with his eyes on other jobs, Allen actually signed on to become a football assistant at Illinois in 1915, only to have the offer withdrawn because of World War I. Finally, in 1919, Allen stepped down and a second tenure at Kansas, one that would make him a legend, was about to begin.

But basketball isn't what lured him back to Lawrence. Allen was hired as the school's athletic director for a $3,500 salary, and four months into the job he faced his first crisis.

Karl Schlademan, the track coach, was assigned the basketball coaching job for 1919-20, but he resigned after one game, saying it was impossible to coach both sports. There was no time to launch a search, and Allen, who was coaching the freshmen team, appointed himself as successor.

In the years immediately after World War I, Kansas played second fiddle to Missouri. Doc Meanwell had interrupted his career at Wisconsin and led the Tigers to league championships in 1918 and 1920. Beating Missouri and Meanwell became Allen's mission.

And in his second KU tenure Allen failed in his first nine attempts. Meanwell was the game's top coach, compiling a 126-11 record and six conference titles in his first eight years, and Allen envied his success. Meanwell returned to Wisconsin after the 1920 season, but Missouri didn't drop off under its new coach, former player Craig Ruby.

Finally, Kansas defeated Missouri in 1922 and the teams tied for the Missouri Valley championship, and 1923 proved to be a pivotal year for Allen and the program because it may have saved his career.

Kansas swept the season series from Missouri and went 16-0 in conference play, and some 15 years later Allen revealed that he had been prepared to turn over the coaching reigns if his 1923 team led by Hall of Fame guard Paul Endacott hadn't surpassed Missouri in league supremacy.

Allen knew this was his best team and Allen's wife, Bessie, told Endacott during a team reunion in 1938 that Allen was prepared to step down without an outright championship. "I don't know if he would have gone through with it," Endacott said. "But that's what Bessie Allen told me and I believe it."

The 1923 team photo is among the most famous in the game's history. The shot includes Allen and Naismith, whom Allen asked to sit in on team pictures, side by side. A third Hall of Fame member is Endacott holding the basketball, and on the fourth row is seldom-used guard Adolph

Rupp, who would become the legendary coach at Kentucky.

The Helms Foundation retroactively named the 1922 and 1923 Jayhawks national champions and banners in Allen Field House today attest to the honor. Nearly three decades would pass before Kansas and Allen again stood atop the basketball world.

There were plenty of highlights along the way to the 1952 NCAA title team. In 1936, the Jayhawks went 18-0 and played for the right to become the first Olympic team before losing a playoff series to Utah State.

The first NCAA Tournament in 1939 was a financial bust in Evanston, Illinois. Allen brought the event to Kansas City in 1940, got his team to the final before a sold out Municipal Auditorium and kept the tournament in business.

After World War II, the state's enthusiasm for basketball had shifted to Kansas State. Coach Jack Gardner got the Wildcats to their first NCAA Tournament in 1948 and they reached the national semifinals. In 1950, the school opened 14,000-seat Ahearn Field House and suddenly Kansas started looking like a second-class basketball citizen.

But Allen had already started to make some changes. In 1948, he sent assistant Coach Dick Harp around the state to recruit the likes of Bill Hougland, Bill Lienhard and Bob Kenney. The sales pitch: Come to Kansas and you'll win the 1952 NCAA championship and an Olympic gold medal.

Allen got the most important player himself.

The 6'9" Lovellette had no intention of leaving Indiana, but Allen wouldn't take no for an answer. He had landed his biggest recruit and now had to make good on his championship promise.

Kansas tied K-State and Nebraska for the 1950 Big Seven title with Lovellette leading the league in scoring as a sophomore. K-State had one of its best teams in 1951, losing the national championship game to Kentucky, and that set the stage for 1952.

Heading into that season, Kansas State had won 10 of the past 12 meetings with Kansas.

K-State did it again, beating the Jayhawks by 17, and KU made it two straight losses by falling at Oklahoma State. Kansas wasn't looking like title timber. The team returned from Stillwater and Allen decided to become a pressing team.

"We had a new enthusiasm, a new perspective," Harp said.

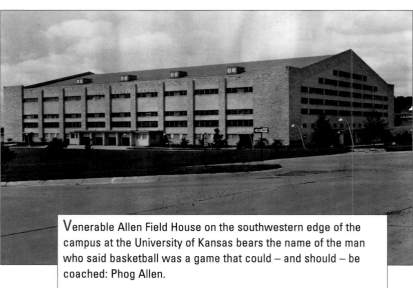

Venerable Allen Field House on the southwestern edge of the campus at the University of Kansas bears the name of the man who said basketball was a game that could – and should – be coached: Phog Allen.

Kansas went on a tear, blowing through the rest of their Big Seven schedule, highlighted by a 17-point victory over Kansas State.

In the NCAA Tournament, the Jayhawks got by TCU by four, and behind Lovellette's 44 points, blitzed St. Louis. For the first time, the NCAA brought all four national semifinalists to one site, creating the first true final four in Seattle.

Second-ranked Illinois was favored to win it all but Kansas was the sentimental choice because of Allen.

He was 66 years old and knew because of the state's retirement recommendation he would have only four more seasons to coach. Allen was proud of his team's achievements in 1922 and 1923 but the Jayhawks had never won a postseason tournament. This would be his best opportunity.

And it came easily. Lovellette scored 33 as Kansas rolled past Santa Clara in the semifinal, and the title game against St. John's wasn't close. Again, Lovellette got 33 and the Jayhawks romped to an 80-63 triumph. Lovellette remains the only person to lead the nation in scoring while playing for a national championship team.

For a coach who contributed so much to the game, the NCAA title stands as the crowning achievement, although Allen had his sites set on the bigger stage of the Olympic Games in Helsinki, Finland.

Still, this was important. Without it, Allen would be remembered as the greatest coach never to win an NCAA championship.

In the Olympic playoffs, Kansas lost in the final to the AAU champion Peoria Caterpillar Diesels. But by reaching the final game, the Jayhawks filled half of the Olympic roster and Allen became the assistant coach for the gold-medal winning team.

The promise was kept.

Allen's Jayhawks were a missed shot away from making it two straight titles as they fell to Indiana by one in the 1953 title game. That game marked the final college contest for a reserve guard, Dean Smith.

Allen's legacy lived on through Smith at North Carolina as it did through Rupp at Kentucky and many other coaches who, because of Allen, can trace their roots to the game's originator who didn't think basketball could or should be coached.

The ABA: Red, White, and Wow

By Terry Pluto

The American Basketball Association?

When some fans hear the name of the league that dueled with the NBA for players and public attention from 1967-76, they think of Julius Erving. Or Marvin Barnes, who once missed a team flight, rented a helicopter to take him to the road game, and arrived at the arena wearing a full-length mink coat with his uniform on underneath. As the trainer taped his ankles for the game, he munched on some McDonald's

Julius "Dr. J" Erving

burgers and fries that he had picked up en route from the helicopter landing strip to the arena.

Or perhaps they think of Spencer Haywood becoming the first player to leave college early and turn pro. Or maybe even the league that gave Bob Costas his first broadcasting job. Or where Hubie Brown and Larry Brown first became professional head coaches. Or the three-point shot. Or the Slam Dunk contest. Or cheerleaders in bikinis in Miami, or a cow-milking contest at halftime of a game in Indiana.

The Denver Nuggets, Indiana Pacers, San Antonio Spurs and New Jersey Nets all began in the ABA. So did Hall of Famers Moses Malone, George Gervin, Dan Issel and David Thompson. The season after those four ABA teams merged into the NBA in 1976-77, five of the 10 starters in the NBA Finals that year between Portland and Philadelphia had played in the ABA. Four of the top 10 NBA scorers that first season after the merger had ABA roots, as did nine players who appeared in the All-Star game.

"At first, the NBA players were very skeptical about us," recalled Issel. "We had to prove we belonged, and we did just that. The only thing I wish was that there were more survivors from the ABA instead of just the four teams that got in."

But even before all that, there was the red, white and blue ball.

"It looks like it belongs on the nose of a seal," said veteran NBA coach Alex Hannum.

Yes, that wild, outrageous, creative, sometimes chaotic collection of athletes, coaches, owners, and teams at times seemed a bit like a circus.

Larry Brown

Ah, yes, the ball.

Now, it's common to see basketballs of nearly all color schemes at local playgrounds and recreation centers. But in the middle 1960s, there was one ball. A boring brown ball. A ball that a man named George Mikan had trouble seeing through the thick lenses of his black horned-rimmed glasses as he watched basketball on his black-and-white television. Mikan is a member of the Hall of Fame and was voted one of the NBA's greatest players of the first half of the 20th century. He was a star with the old Minneapolis Lakers. He was 6'10", had a law degree, and owned a travel agency in Minneapolis. When the new owners were trying to put the ABA together and needed a commissioner, they called Mikan and …

Wait a minute, we're talking about the ABA. When you do that, one story leads to another. So before it can be told how an NBA icon became the commissioner of what appeared to be a renegade league and then insisted on a red, white and blue ball, understand this about the ABA - it was supposed to be a football league!

If anyone is to be credited with starting the ABA, it's a man named Dennis Murphy. He put together some investors to try to buy an American Football League franchise and bring it to Orange County, California. Their goal was to bite off a piece of the old AFL because they believed the National Football League was about to swallow that league. They'd either end up with a valuable NFL franchise, or the NFL would buy them out when the leagues merged. But that deal fell through.

"We had a pretty good group of money people who loved sports, and we thought they should do something," said Murphy. "I thought how there was only one (major) hockey league and one basketball league. I knew nothing about hockey, but basketball was my favorite sport. That was my reasoning: I liked basketball better than hockey. No surveys, nothing like they'd do today. The NBA had only 12 teams in 1966. It seemed like there should be more. Why? I don't know. It was worth a shot, and the AFL worked."

It's a very long story about how all the investors came and went before the first red, white and blue ball ever went through the net for three points (yet another story to come). A group of daring young men such as Murphy, Dick Tinkham, Mike Storen, Gary Davidson, Gabe Rubin and others pulled together enough cash to field 11 teams from Anaheim to Minneapolis to New Jersey. Before he became famous as a shock talk show host, Morton Downey Jr. was acting as general manager of the New Orleans franchise, and he actually signed Larry Brown and Doug Moe to play for the new Bucs. Singer Pat Boone was hustled into buying part of the Oakland franchise. Bill Ringsby owned the Denver franchise, which he called The Rockets, named after his Rocket trucking company. The team logo matched that which was painted on the side of his trucks.

Back to Mikan. They called him at his Minneapolis travel agency. Mikan really did get the ABA going. He was a huge name, and could attract media attention and investors. He also thought the league needed a symbol.

"It was the American Basketball Association," said Mikan. "What color is the American flag? Red, white, and blue. So why not have a red, white, and blue ball?"

As the Godfather of the new league, when Mikan spoke, it came into being. The ball was

> "It was the American Basketball Association. What color is the American flag? Red, white, and blue. So why not have a red, white, and blue ball?"
>
> — George Mikan

indeed red, white, and blue. There were a few problems: there were no red, white, and blue balls in production. So the Indiana Pacers painted some brown balls red, white, and blue. It was as if the balls were a huge, round, slippery piece of soap, resulting in 44 turnovers in the first half of an exhibition game at Denver.

Once they made balls that felt like basketballs should, some in the ABA began shooting them from spots on the court no one ever dreamed players would. That's because the league added the 3-point shot, originally used in the American Basketball League in the early 1960s. Some of the owners of the new ABA were aware that the old ABL awarded three points for a shot made behind an arc that was supposed to be 25 feet from the basket above the top of the key, and about 22 feet from the corners. It was designed to create a role for the smaller, more skilled outside shooter. It also was to help open up the middle of the court so it would make it easier to drive down the lane. In the NBA, the temptation was to give the opposition the long jump shot because the odds were that he'd miss it.

The 3-pointer changed the math. You could go 2-of-6 from three-point range (33 percent), and that was the same as 3-of-6 (50 percent) from two-point range. It created some great shooters, such as Kentucky's Louie Dampier. But there were guys such as Les Selvage ("He acted like if he stepped over the 3-point line, he was going to get killed for something," said veteran ABA coach Bob Bass. "He didn't just shoot 25-footers, he shot 30-footers"). Selvage was working as a shipping clerk for Douglas Aircraft when he tried out for the Anaheim Amigos. Selvage made the team and then proved night after night that he certainly was a shooter … if not always a scorer. He heaved up a mind-numbing total of 461 3-pointers, not just more than any ABA player. It was more than any TEAM except Pittsburgh. He made 32 percent, averaged 13.2 points, his team won only 25 games and his career lasted only that one year.

But the power of the 3-pointer prevailed. Coaching in Kentucky, Hubie Brown set up plays for 6' Louie Dampier to shoot

3-pointers off fast breaks and in-bounds passes. Like Indiana's Mel Daniels and Roger Brown, Dampier's career is lost under all the dust of ABA history. Many from the ABA who saw a lot of Dampier, Brown and Daniels believe all three could have been Hall of Famers had the primes of their careers been spent in the NBA.

When the ABA began in 1967, there were only a dozen NBA teams. With 12 players on a roster, there were only 144 professional basketball players in the United States. There were no European leagues, nothing else but Industrial League basketball with teams such as the Akron Goodyears and Phillips 66ers. So it wasn't hard to find talent. Rather than being diluted by expansion, as much of pro sports is today, the stew was thick with promising possibilities for general

The ABA's Kentucky Colonels had "best chance" draft rights to Dan Issel.

Pete Maravich was a ball-handling magician at LSU.

managers and coaches willing to dip into the pot a bit and spoon it out. Connie Hawkins had been banned from the NBA because of alleged point-shaving involvement. Others were also tainted. Commissioner Mikan "investigated" and determined there was no proof of any wrongdoing by Hawkins or anyone else. The ABA extended a hand like the Statue of Liberty, willing to give almost anyone a chance at a pro basketball dream. Playground legends, top college players who were rejected by the NBA and older guys from the industrial leagues all found a home, especially in the first few years. It didn't take long to see that the league had talent, even if the NBA was not about to admit it.

The ABA arrived at just the right time because pro basketball was underexposed, poorly marketed and sometimes ignored in a few cities where it ranked not only behind professional baseball and football, but also behind big time college athletics. On national television in the 1960s, the NBA Game of the Week often was the Boston Celtics vs. whichever team had Wilt Chamberlain. For most players, salaries were low, options were few. There was no free agency as we know it today, nor any international market for their skills. A player could not turn pro until his college class graduated, so Chamberlain spent a season with the Globetrotters between his time at Kansas and the beginning of his NBA career in Philadelphia.

The ABA changed all that. At first, it signed players ignored by the NBA. Then they went after players in the NBA, the first big name being Rick Barry. He was chastised for jumping from the NBA's San Francisco Warriors to the ABA's Oakland Oaks. He was considered "disloyal,"

Kareem Abdul-Jabbar

but consider Barry's situation. He was 23 years old, and had just finished his second pro season, averaging 35 points to lead the league in scoring for a team that went to the NBA Finals. He had a base salary of $30,000 and earned a $15,000 bonus for the 1966-67 season. His contract had expired, although the NBA would later claim in court that despite his contract being up, he was still tied to the Warriors for five years under something called the reserve clause. Yes, Barry received what seemed to be a better deal from Oakland — $75,000 plus 15 percent ownership in the team, but the Warriors would eventually match it.

A story seldom told is that Oakland had just hired Bruce Hale as its first coach. He also had coached Barry at the University of Miami. And he also happened to be Barry's father-in-law. And when it came to deciding between Oakland and San Francisco, Barry was facing pressure encountered by few players.

"People said I signed with Oakland because Pat Boone was one of the owners and he promised to get me into the movies," said Barry. "That was a bunch of bull. The main thing was my family, sharing basketball with them and playing for Bruce Hale. I made the jump for $30,000 (more) a year and a piece of the fledging franchise that may not have been worth anything, and it turned out it wasn't worth a dime to me."

Mikan had advised each ABA team to sign an established NBA star such as Barry, then the ABA planned to sue the NBA on behalf of the players claiming the league was restraining trade. But only Oakland did so in that first season, and lawsuits kept Barry off the court for a year.

The NBA hated the ABA for a variety of reasons, but the biggest was money. The new league was rocking the boat of the financial structure that gave the NBA tremendous leverage over its players. It's our league, our arenas, our ball and if you don't like it, go get a job somewhere else, knowing there was nowhere else for a pro basketball player to go. Then came the ABA. Then Barry jumped leagues. Later, stars such as Billy Cunningham, Zelmo Beaty and Joe Caldwell followed. Even officials Earl Strom, Joe Gushue, John Vanak and Norm Drucker jumped from the NBA to the ABA. The ABA's goal wasn't just to have better players and officials, it was to hurt the NBA. They wanted to drive up the NBA's cost of doing business so that the old league would have no choice but to take in at least some of the teams from the new league.

When it came time to draft players, the ABA allowed any franchise that it thought had the best chance of signing a certain college star to have the draft rights. So Purdue shooting guard Rick Mount was courted by the Indiana Pacers. The draft rights to University of Kentucky star Dan Issel were awarded to the Kentucky Colonels. The idea wasn't for the ABA teams to defeat each other. Yes, they wanted to win, but more importantly, the ABA wanted to prevail in any duel with the NBA. Every time a big college name such as Issel, Mount, Artis Gilmore or Len Elmore picked an ABA franchise over the NBA, it was viewed as a victory for the entire league. It also raised the price of college players such as Pete Maravich or Kareem Abdul-Jabbar (then

Lew Alcindor) when they finally did sign out of college with an NBA franchise.

Even more than the incorporation of the 3-point shot by the ABA, a decision made by the league that really did change the pro game was the signing of Olympic hero Spencer Haywood after his sophomore year at the University of Detroit, where he averaged 32 points and 22 rebounds.

It was the summer of 1969, and Haywood knew his future was pro basketball. Why go back to college? An agent named Steve Arnold asked, "Why did Haywood have to stay in college for four years?"

Or as Arnold explained, "There was this silent partnership between the NBA and the NCAA. The NBA agreed not to touch players until their college eligibility was up. That way, the colleges could make money off them. The colleges gave the NBA a free farm system so the players could develop their skills for four years and then there was an orderly way for those players to turn pro – the NBA draft – with the NBA not having to worry about anyone else competing for the players' services."

The ABA decided this was unfair, a restraint of trade and also a good way to upset the NBA – which mattered most. So they signed Haywood after his sophomore season to play for Denver, where he averaged 30 points and 19.5 rebounds (he was, indeed, ready for the pros). The New York Nets signed Jim Chones out of Marquette after his junior year. University of Indiana sophomore George McGinnis signed with the Pacers. All those moves made headlines, and Haywood also inspired lawsuits.

Then the ABA signed a junior from the University of Massachusetts named Julius Erving. The signing was utterly ignored by the media and most of the basketball world. Virginia Squires general manager Johnny Kerr and coach Al Bianchi had a grainy black-and-white film of Erving against North Carolina in a National Invitational Tournament game. They had a word from former Celtic star Bob Cousy that "this kid from UMass was pretty good." They had Squires owner Earl Foreman, who knew that Erving worked at a summer camp where his son attended, and Foreman "called my kid's camp counselor, who was an assistant football coach at Bates College."

Foreman asked him about Erving, and the assistant football coach said, "Forget Cousy, forget everybody. Julius Erving is the greatest player to ever come out of New England." His agent also was Steve Arnold, who was convincing players to leave school early – and Arnold said only the Squires had interest in a guy who later became a legend. This was still an era when there were glittering stars in college, but pros still missed them. It was before cable television, before the Internet, before all the scouting services and when most teams had only one or two scouts on the payroll. It was when teams took *Street & Smith's Basketball Preview Magazine* into their draft rooms to cross-check college players. It's why the ABA could pressure the NBA. There were good players everywhere, just longing for a chance to turn pro – and some of them not wanting to wait four years for their college class to graduate. The ABA even signed Moses Malone straight out of high school. Eventually, the NBA had to sign players early, too. Through it all, the price of the athletes rose, and the bottom lines for teams in both leagues were bleeding red as owners and accountants agonized over all the bills.

After nine years, it was over. Both leagues knew it. The players knew it. The agents hated the idea of it because they had become influential (and

> "We saw so many of our players do well after the merger, and we could only say to the world, 'We told you so.'"
> — Bob Costas.

sometimes very wealthy) as the two leagues battled to sign players. There had to be a merger. There no longer were questions that the ABA had NBA talent. Too many players who had dribbled the NBA's brown ball and the ABA's red, white and blue version could testify to that fact. As Rick Barry said, "The best thing about the ABA was the players." Consider that hardly anyone knew about George Gervin when he signed with Virginia at the age of 19 and had

played only one year at Eastern Michigan. Think about it: Erving, Gervin, Issel, Malone, Connie Hawkins and David Thompson all began in the ABA and ended up in the Hall of Fame. So did a couple of coaches named Hubie Brown and Larry Brown.

In the middle of the 1975-76 season, the ABA had an event that later inspired the NBA's All-Star weekend. Three ABA teams had folded. The league was down to seven teams and one division. Denver was a powerhouse featuring Thompson, Issel and Bobby Jones with Larry Brown coaching, aided by assistant Doug Moe. The league decided to play the game in Denver with the Nuggets facing an All-Star collection composed of players from the other six teams. They hired country singers Charlie Rich and Glen Campbell to supply the entertainment. They wanted something different, something to excite the fans. In a brain-storming session, the Nuggets public relations man said that the ABA was famous for its dunkers, so why not have a Slam Dunk contest?

Nuggets general manager Carl Scheer, ABA league official Jim Keeler and some others in the meeting loved the idea – but had no clue how to run a Slam Dunk Contest. They finally made up a few rules. They picked the dunkers from the Nuggets and the All-Stars because they didn't want to pay extra expenses to bring in other players. The winner would receive $1,000 and a stereo system. The five who took part were Erving, Thompson, Gilmore, Gervin and Larry Kenon. They knew it would come down to a duel between Thompson and Erving, which Erving eventually won with a dunk where legend has it that he took off from the foul line and soared to the rim. Films actually show it was about six inches beyond the line, but that still means he covered more than 14 feet in the air. "I did step on the foul line, as Doug Moe was quick to point out," recalled Erving. "I said to Doug, 'I'm not doing that again. No one else can dunk from anywhere near out as far as I just did.'"

In the end, four ABA teams were admitted to the NBA as "expansion" teams: Denver, San Antonio, Indiana and the New York Nets for the 1976-77 season. Each had to pay the NBA $3.2 million. The Nets had to pay the New York Knicks $4.8 million for indemnification, for playing in their basketball territory. That led to the Nets having to sell Erving to the Philadelphia 76ers for $3 million, so the Nets could buy their way into the NBA.

Two other ABA franchises remained in business – Kentucky and St. Louis. The NBA did not want them, and the other ABA owners had to cut a deal for them to fold if the merger were to succeed. John Y. Brown received $3 million from the ABA owners to fold his Kentucky Colonels franchise. Brown then bought into the NBA by purchasing the Buffalo Braves for $1.5 million.

That left the St. Louis Spirits, owned by brothers Ozzie and Danny Silna along with Don Schupak. They were paid $2.2 million in cash. In a move of pure financial genius, they agreed to take a 1/7th share of the annual TV revenue from each of the four teams admitted to the NBA – in perpetuity, meaning forever! They are still receiving a cut each year from San Antonio, Indiana, Denver and the Nets. Since 1976, they have pocketed countless millions for a team that they owned for only two years without a winning record.

The ABA was a league of schemers, dreamers and deal makers. And among that group, no one made a better deal than the owners of the St. Louis Spirits. No new league will ever have the impact or the tremendous talent level that the ABA brought to the NBA. No established league will probably ever adopt as many ideas from a new league, as the NBA did when importing everything from the 3-point shot to dancing cheerleaders to the Slam Dunk contest to even keeping stats for things such as blocked shots, steals and turnovers.

"The ABA had a split personality," recalled Bob Costas, who called the Spirits games for two years. "On the one hand, the ABA people knew what a great thing they had, how talented their players were and how entertaining. It was almost as if we didn't want to share our secret with the rest of the world. Yet there was such pride in a league that had to endure so much simply to survive, and we wanted the world to know how great our players were."

And it didn't take long for the NBA and its fans to see just that as Denver won the Midwest Division, San Antonio had a 44-38 record, and nine players in the 1977 All-Star Game had begun their careers in the ABA.

"We saw so many of our players do well after the merger, and we could only say to the world, 'We told you so,'" said Costas.

They Got Next

By Mel Greenberg

In 1969, a novel plan was hatched when West Chester University women's coach Carol Eckman decided it would be neat if a tournament were held that consisted of collegiate teams exclusively for the first time to play for a national title. Until then, AAU teams were mixed with collegiate programs.

And so Eckman went about handing invitations to a bunch of schools to come participate in the event, from which her Golden Rams emerged victorious.

It worked out so well, however, that two more were held in ensuing seasons with future Naismith Memorial Basketball Hall of Famer Billie Moore (1999) coaching Cal-State Fullerton to one of those titles.

In 1972, the National Association of Girls and Women in Sport launched a tournament at Illinois State that was held under the auspices of the newly formed Association for Intercollegiate Athletics for Women (AIAW).

Immaculata, coached by 2008 Naismith Hall of Famer Cathy Rush in suburban Philadelphia, won that AIAW title and two more through 1974 to launch what can be considered the start of the modern era of the women's game.

Since then, many events have happened to bring the women's game to where it is today. Let's take a tour of more than three decades of people, places and noteworthy moments:

Several individuals enshrined in the Hall of Fame achieved their success as early pioneers that blazed a trail to the current era.

Three became the first women inducted: Senda Berenson Abbott, as a contributor for adopting Dr. Naismith's rules at Smith College in 1892; Bertha P. Teague, as a contributor and as a successful high school coach in Ada, Oklahoma, and whose record at Byng High School in 42 years was 1,157-115; and L. Margaret Wade, who coached at Delta State in the 1970s, but then after the program was revived years later, succeeded Immaculata in winning the next three AIAW titles (1975-77).

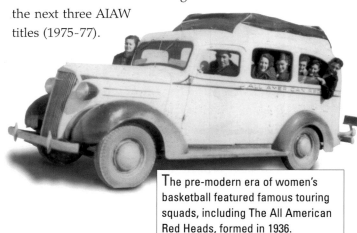

The pre-modern era of women's basketball featured famous touring squads, including The All American Red Heads, formed in 1936.

The pre-modern era also featured two famous touring squads – The All American Red Heads, formed in 1936, and the Wayland Baptist Flying Queens out of Texas, who flew around the country and also played in the early AIAW tournaments, advancing deep several times.

Two other events in the 1970s helped spur the women's game as we know it today – one was the passage of Title IX that set the stage for athletic scholarships for women, and the other was the move to a five-player, full-court game for women.

In 1978, the AIAW tournament format changed, with regional advancement to a Final Four, similar to the NCAA. UCLA, which hosted the event, won the title under Billie Moore.

The Bruins had two stars who later became Hall of Famers: Ann Meyers (1993), the first four-time All-American in the women's game who was given an NBA tryout by the Indianapolis Pacers and was later a WNBA general manager with the Phoenix Mercury; and Denise Curry (1997).

That Final Four also had Wayland Baptist, Maryland, and Montclair State, which had a scoring sensation in Carol Blazejowski, a 1994 inductee who has been in the front office of the WNBA's New York Liberty since the team's inception in 1997.

In 1976 the *Philadelphia Inquirer* launched a weekly Top 20 collegiate poll that two years later formulated under the auspices of the Associated Press. It began as a coaches poll, later expanded to 25 teams, and in 1994-95 became a media poll, which it remains today.

The Olympics introduced women's basketball in the Montreal Games in 1976 and the United States, coached by Billie Moore, won a silver medal finishing second to a Soviet team led by 7'2" Uljana Semjonova, a 1993 inductee and one of two foreign women enshrined in Springfield.

The other is former Brazilian star Hortencia Marcari, a 2005 inductee.

Three notables on the first U.S. Olympic team were a teenager named Nancy Leiberman, who could be considered the first to put people in the seats to watch women play, UCLA's Meyers, and Pat Summitt, who was also starting out as a coach at Tennessee. The Vols quickly became a dominant program in which Summitt, in 2009, became the first men's or women's coach to win more than 1,000 collegiate games. She also has won eight NCAA titles.

Leiberman is a 1996 Naismith inductee, while Summitt, who coached USA to a gold medal in 1984 at the Los Angeles games, was enshrined in 2000.

In 1979 and 1980, Old Dominion, coached by former Immaculata star Marianne Stanley, won back-to-back AIAW titles with Leiberman as a member.

In 1980, ODU added 6'8" Anne Donovan, a 1995 inductee who later became a two-time Olympic gold medalist. The native of Ridgewood, New Jersey, later became a successful coach, leading the Seattle Storm to the 2004 WNBA title and then coaching USA to an Olympic gold medal in

Early women's basketball resembled dance or exercise classes.

Beijing in 2008. She became a New York Liberty assistant in 2009.

The United States did not participate in the 1980 Olympics because of the boycott imposed by President Jimmy Carter. But the coach was Sue Gunter, a 2005 inductee who had a successful coaching career at Stephen F. Austin and then at LSU, winning more than 800 games.

In 1981, Louisiana Tech won the AIAW title. Leon Barmore was then an assistant to Sonja Hogg but he later became a co-head coach and then took over the program outright, earning several more titles and becoming a Naismith Hall of Famer in 2003. He came out of retirement in 2008-09 to become an assistant to his former Techsters star Kim Mulkey at Baylor, where she had led the Bears to the 2005 NCAA title.

The NCAA came on the scene for women in 1981-82 with the Techsters winning the first title, while Rutgers, under former Immaculata star Theresa Grentz, defeated Texas in the final AIAW tournament. The first NCAA Final Four also had Summitt's Tennessee team and Cheyney out of suburban Philadelphia, coached by C. Vivian Stringer, the 2009 Naismith inductee from the women's ranks.

Stringer went on to win more than 800 games and became the first men's or women's coach to lead three different teams to the Final Four. Her Iowa team reached the finals in 1993. She then led Rutgers to a Final Four in 2000 and again in 2007 when the Scarlet Knights lost in the title game to Tennessee.

The next two years (1983-84) belonged to Southern Cal, featuring a dynamic player in Cheryl Miller, the younger sister of NBA star Reggie Miller. She, too, put people in the seats, won an Olympic gold medal and became a 1995 inductee.

The early '80s also featured another scoring sensation in Lynette Woodard, a 2004 inductee who played for Kansas and became the first female to play for the Harlem Globetrotters.

In 1986, Texas became the first NCAA unbeaten champion at 34-0. The Longhorns were coached by Jody Conradt, a 1998 inductee who also was a 900-game winner.

That year also saw Nancy Leiberman become the first woman to play in a men's professional league when she joined the USBL's Springfield Fame in the Hall's backyard.

Texas was the host of the first NCAA Final Four sellout in 1987 when Tennessee earned its first national title. The tournament crowds continued to grow and several events were held in domed stadiums.

In 1988, the United States earned its second Olympic gold but first without the games

Did You Know?

1892: The first rules for the game were published in the Springfield College school newspaper, *The Triangle*.

1895: The original 20-foot free throw line was moved to 15 feet from the basket for the 1894-95 season.

Beginning with the 1895-96 men's season, a field goal is changed from 1 to 2 points and a free throw is changed from 3 to 1 point. Five-man teams become standard.

The WNBA has given the college game's best players an avenue to continue their basketball careers.

tainted by boycotts from either the Russians or Americans. North Carolina State's Kay Yow, a 2002 Naismith inductee, was the USA coach. In January of 2009, Yow lost a courageous battle against breast cancer. The Women's Basketball Coaches Association set up a foundation to fight the disease.

One of the first recipients in 1992 along with Nera White was former Delta State star Lusia Harris-Stewart, who in 1977 became the first woman drafted by an NBA team when the former New Orleans Jazz selected her.

In 1994 one of the most exciting NCAA title games occurred with North Carolina rallying to beat Louisiana Tech when Charlotte Smith sank a three-pointer at the buzzer.

Meanwhile, a new program was gaining momentum out of the Northeast in the wake of its first Final Four appearance in 1991.

Early in the 1995 season, Connecticut rose to challenge Tennessee's supremacy, beating the Vols in a landmark game in Storrs in January and then beating Summitt's bunch in the NCAA championship, finishing unbeaten and setting up a heated national rivalry that lasted until Summitt cancelled the series in the summer of 2007.

Huskies coach Geno Auriemma went on to gain enshrinement in 2006. He has now led UConn to six national titles, including a third unbeaten run in 2009, which was capped a week later when Auriemma was named to coach the USA women in the 2012 Olympic games in London.

Stars from Connecticut's program have included Rebecca Lobo, Sue Bird, and Diana Taurasi, all of whom have potential to earn enshrinement in Springfield in the future.

At Tennessee, some former Vols stars with the same stature include Chamique Holdsclaw, a member of the 1998 unbeaten champions, and Candace Parker, who in 2008 was both the top WNBA rookie and MVP, playing for the Los Angeles Sparks.

The Tennessee-Connecticut rivalry helped gain more TV interest in the women's game and now ESPN airs every contest in the NCAA tournament.

The tournament, which began with a field of 24 teams, continued to expand to eventually reach 64 and to allow each conference to place its champion in the field.

In 1996, Stanford coach Tara VanDerveer led a year-long effort to win a gold medal at the Atlanta Olympic games, providing impetus for two pro leagues. Although the American Basketball League joined earlier failed efforts at pro ball in the United States after a two-year run, the NBA spawned the WNBA, to be played in the summer beginning in 1997 and the pro league made it to season number 13 in 2009.

Beginning with eight teams, the league grew to 16 but has since scaled back.

The Houston Comets, who folded in the winter of 2008, won the first four titles, coached by former Mississippi mentor Van Chancellor. He went on to lead USA to the 2004 Olympic gold medal in Athens, Greece, and earned enshrinement in 2007.

Who will be the next big story in the evolution of the women's game?

Who will become the next Hall of Famer?

Stars from Connecticut's program include Rebecca Lobo.

The Houston Comets won the first four WNBA titles.

TREASURES OF THE HALL OF FAME

The Naismith Memorial

Basketball Hall of Fame

shows off some of its most

hallowed artifacts.

Looking Back

Since 1959, the Naismith Memorial Basketball Hall of Fame has honored and celebrated the game's greatest moments and brightest stars. On the occasion of its 50th Anniversary, we look back as the greatest shrine to the greatest game fulfills its steadfast promise to be the world's finest sports museum.

The Naismith Memorial Basketball Hall of Fame is home to nearly three hundred inductees and more than 40,000 square feet of basketball history. The following pages contain only a small portion of the greatest basketball memorabilia in the world.

The magnificent interior of the Hall of Fame's dome.

Interactive exhibits enhance visitors' experiences.

Within the Hall is Center Court, an iconic, breathtaking, full-size regulation basketball court where the game never ends. On any given day, visitors lace 'em up to play under the basketball heavens, reliving the glory days of yesteryear or practicing for the big games yet to come.

The landmark structure is one of the world's most distinctive monuments punctuating the Springfield skyline and stirring the spirits of basketball fans everywhere.

Piece of flooring from the original gymnasium (pictured right) where basketball was first played on December 21, 1891, at the YMCA International Training School in Springfield, Massachusetts.

"The Larry" - Named after former NBA commissioner Larry O'Brien. Hoisting the NBA championship trophy becomes the defining moment in the careers of many Hall of Famers.

The first team to make the green shamrock strike fear in the eyes of opponents was the Original Celtics of New York. This barnstorming squad was one of the finest teams ever assembled. The lineup included future Hall of Famers John Beckman, Dutch Dehnert, Nat Holman, and Joe Lapchick.

James Naismith invented basketball in 1891 shortly after his 30th birthday. More than 100 years later, the game is still his gift to the world, yet only a few remnants of Naismith's basketball life endure to the present day.

Before Notre Dame snapped UCLA's 88-game winning streak in 1974, John Wooden's Bruins defeated the Fighting Irish 82-63 to run UCLA's winning streak to 61 games, surpassing the previous record of 60 held by the University of San Francisco.

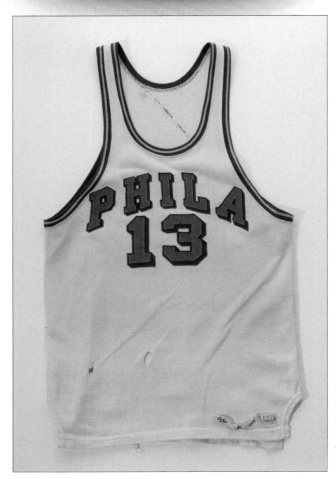

Meadowlark Lemon worked "The Magic Circle" for the famed Harlem Globetrotters for more than 20 years. Lemon entertained fans around the world with his unique brand of basketball that included hook shots from half-court and beyond.

On March 2, 1962, Wilt Chamberlain did the unthinkable when he scored 100 points in an NBA game. The Big Dipper wore this jersey on that historic night in Hershey, PA.

Tennessee's Pat Summitt has won more than 1,000 games in her distinguished career. Her Lady Vols helped catapult women's basketball into the mainstream and her eight NCAA national championships rank her second only to John Wooden. This is one of her game-day jackets.

Basketball's earliest uniforms included wool tops and padded shorts, while the first basketballs included laces that made dribbling hazardous on any playing surface.

Kobe Bryant scored 81 points against the Toronto Raptors on January 22, 2006. Bryant, a four-time NBA champion, wore these signature shoes that historic night.

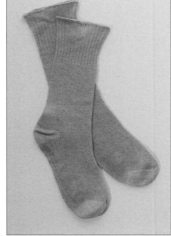

Pete Maravich wore these floppy grey socks on his way to scoring 3,667 points at LSU. "Pistol" was one of the game's true originals, showcasing his incredible basketball talent with a level of showmanship few others possess.

The first real superstar of basketball? None other than the bespectacled George Mikan. Mikan was the game's first dominant big man and he led the Minneapolis Lakers to five championships in six years from 1948 to 1954.

Syracuse Nationals owner Danny Biasone came up with the idea of the 24-second shot clock in 1954.

The UCLA Bruins won ten NCAA national championships under Coach John Wooden. Kareem Abdul-Jabbar, then Lew Alcindor, dominated the collegiate game, leading the Bruins to three consecutive national titles from 1967 to 1969.

In 1965, it cost $7 to attend an NCAA tournament game. In recent years, ticket prices have gone into the thousands of dollars.

The United States continued its dominance in international competition winning the gold medal at the 1952 Olympic Games in Helsinki, Finland.

The 1992 NBA All-Star Game was one for the ages as Magic Johnson came out of retirement to steal the show. Magic really was *magic* that day.

Larry Bird scored his 20,000th career point right where he should have – at home, in Boston Garden.

The game was only 13 years old at the time, but basketball was an exhibition sport at the 1904 World's Fair in St. Louis.

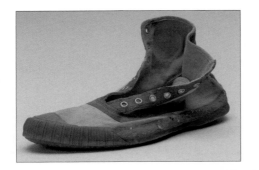

A critically important piece of equipment — the basketball shoe — has evolved with the game.

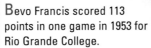

Bevo Francis scored 113 points in one game in 1953 for Rio Grande College.

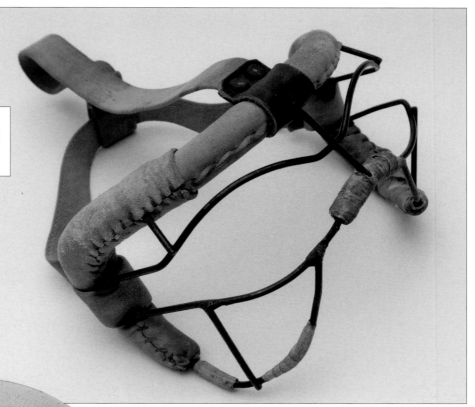

The facemask of the 1950s gave players protection but comfort and visibility were certainly sacrificed.

Wilt ended his career with 31,419 points.

The Bulls went 72-10 in 1995-96.

The Basketball Hall of Fame presents each new Hall of Famer with this ring at the annual Enshrinement Ceremony.

The Walter Brown trophy was presented annually to the NBA champion from 1964 to 1978.

Bill Bradley wore these shorts at Princeton, at a time when baggy was not in!

Lenny Wilkens wore this unisuit jersey at Providence.

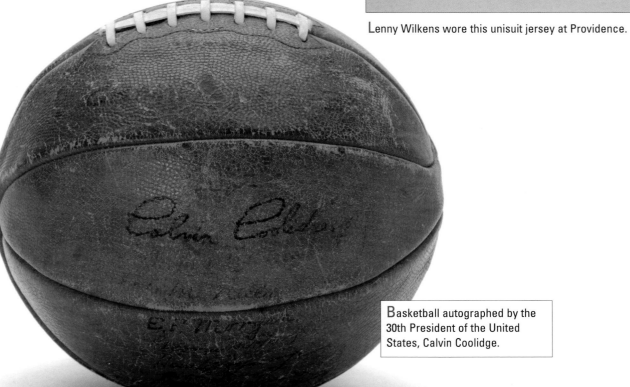

Basketball autographed by the 30th President of the United States, Calvin Coolidge.

Bill Russell

Bill Walton

Another award for Michael Jordan.

Michael Jordan

Chamique Holdsclaw

Bill Bradley

Lebron James

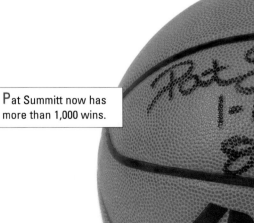

Lisa Leslie

Christian Laettner

Pat Summitt now has more than 1,000 wins.

LEAPS FORWARD

LEAPS FORWARD

From racial integration to global marketing, "Leaps Forward" is about the people, teams, and moments that catapulted basketball from one level to the next.

The Harlem Globetrotters:
The Comedic and Competitive Stylings of Basketball's Greatest Team

By Ben Green

There are a few players in basketball history who are identifiable by one name: Wilt, Oscar, Magic, Bird, Michael, Shaq. But there is only one basketball team that is identifiable by a song. Not even a song, really, but a whistle. All it takes is hearing two or three bars of "Sweet Georgia Brown" and millions of basketball fans think instantly of the Harlem Globetrotters.

The Globetrotters are an iconic institution in basketball history. And not just in the United States, but around the world. In their 80-year history, the Globetrotters have played in 120 countries, and for millions of people the Globetrotters were their first exposure to the game. As NBA Commissioner David Stern said in a 2005 PBS documentary, "When I started traveling the world for the NBA 25 years ago, it was still indelibly imprinted upon nations—when you said basketball, people would say 'Harlem Globetrotters.'"

Ironically, the Globetrotters are so familiar that many fans assume they know everything about the team, just because they've seen them in person or on television. In truth, there are many, many aspects to the Globetrotters' saga that most people don't know. "I had no idea," is the common refrain when people find out. Indeed, one could fill a list called "Facts about the Harlem Globetrotters that No One Knows."

To wit:

Fact #1: The team was born on Chicago's South Side, comprising former players from Wendell Phillips High School, the Giles Post American Legion team, and a local semi-pro team, the Savoy Big Five. Originally known as Tommy Brookins' Globe Trotters, they wanted to get out of Chicago and barnstorm in the Midwest. Brookins knew it would be difficult, if not impossible, for a black man to book games with white teams, so he hired an energetic young promoter, Abe Saperstein, to book a tour of Michigan and

> ## The greatest day I ever spent in basketball was when my father took me to Madison Square Garden to see the Harlem Globetrotters play the College All-Stars.
>
> — Larry Brown

Wisconsin. Eventually, Saperstein took over the team. He added "Harlem" to its name to make sure there was no confusion that this was an African-American team. "Harlem" was like a neon sign advertising black America.

Fact #2: The Globetrotters have been around since the late 1920s. In the early years, it was just five black players and a stumpy Jewish guy in a rattletrap Model T, barnstorming across the American heartland, playing obscure whistle stops and tank towns that no one else would play—Owatonna, Wahpeton, Cut Bank, and Plentywood. They were playing seven nights a week and twice on Sundays, taking on all comers, from the local brake factory team to the smart-aleck college kids, and kicking the white boys' butts—not just beating them, but making fools of them in the process, leaving the crowd laughing in their wake.

Early on, they started adding fancy passing drills and ball-handling tricks at the end of games, first of all to give the players a break from running, and more importantly, to hold down the score so they'd get invited back the next year. The ball-handling eventually became "the show"—the Globetrotters' signature gags and comedy routines.

Their schedule was almost inconceivable: they played 150 games a year, from November through March. They traveled 40,000 miles a year in the dead of winter, in Montana, Minnesota, and the Dakotas, winning 95 percent of their games yet still barely getting by, going hungry on many nights, sometimes driving 200 miles to find a black-owned boarding house or a family that would take them in. The Harlem Globetrotters were not just a great barnstorming team, they were a sociology class on wheels, bringing black hoops and black culture to a hundred Midwestern towns that had seen neither, and in the process transforming Dr. James Naismith's stodgy, wearisome game—which was still sometimes played in chicken-wire cages by roughneck immigrants with flailing elbows and bloodied skulls, a sport more resembling rugby— into an orchestration of speed, fluidity, motion, dazzling skill and, most improbably, inspired comedy.

Fact #3: Despite their humble beginnings, by the mid-1950s the Globetrotters had become the most popular basketball team in the country. In fact, one could argue that they were the most successful sports franchise of any kind, rivaled only by the New York Yankees. In 1950 alone, Saperstein turned down 300 booking requests and put a second Globetrotter squad on the road to meet the demand. The two units played a combined 247 games in 1950-51, and 334 games the next season. By 1954, the Harlem Globetrotters were a year-round operation, with four squads simultaneously traversing the globe.

From 1950-1962, the most popular basketball event in the country was *not* the NBA Finals or the NCAA Championships, but the College All-Star Tour, one of Saperstein's most brilliant pro-

motions. It was a three-week transcontinental series matching the Globetrotters against the top college All-Americans. They played in a different city every night—21 games in 19 nights— selling out every arena, and setting attendance records in dozens of cities, including world records of 31,648 in the Rose Bowl and 36,256 at the Los Angeles Coliseum.

The college All-Americans, who were coached by Ray Meyer and Clair Bee, included the greatest players of that era: Paul Arizin, Bob Cousy, Bill Sharman, Frank Ramsey, Larry Costello, Tom Gola, Jack Twyman, Guy Rodgers, K.C. Jones, Walt Bellamy, Bill Bridges, and Tom Heinsohn.

How big was it? When Larry Brown was inducted into the Naismith Memorial Basketball Hall of Fame in September 2002, he said in his induction speech, "The greatest day I ever spent in basketball was when my father took me to Madison Square Garden to see the Harlem Globetrotters play the College All-Stars."

The popularity of the Globetrotters was enhanced by the dawn of the electronic age. In addition to the legions of fans who saw them in person, millions of others saw them in Movietone and Paramount newsreels and in *two* full-length Hollywood feature films: *The Harlem Globetrotters* in 1951 and *Go, Man, Go!* in 1954.

Fact #4: The Globetrotters were not only the most popular team in the country, but in the late 1940s they were arguably the best. It wasn't that astonishing, really, since Saperstein had a virtual monopoly on the best African-American players in the country. In 1940, the Trotters won the World Pro Tournament, held annually in

Chicago, defeating the best pro teams in the country.

But their greatest triumph, and the most significant game in Globetrotter history, occurred in February 1948, when they beat the NBA's best team, the Minneapolis Lakers, in a head-to-head showdown. Prior to the game, conventional wisdom among sportswriters and bookies was that the Trotters didn't stand a chance. No bunch of "sepia clowns" could stand up to the Lakers' 6' 10" center, George Mikan, the most dominating big man in the game.

But the Globetrotters played the Lakers straight-up, ran them off their feet in the second half, and won on a last-second shot. That win was dismissed as a fluke, but the Trotters did it again the following year, winning by four points, and this time even "put on the show"—beating Mikan and then dancing on his grave. All over America, black families raised up the Trotters as heroes of their race.

Fact #5: The Globetrotters spread the game of basketball around the world. The success of the College All-Stars Tour became a template for world-wide barnstorming. If the Globetrotters could do it across America, why not across Europe? South America? Asia? Why not around the world?

In May 1950, the Trotters made their first of 33 European tours, and took the Old World by storm. As admired as the Trotters were in America, their popularity abroad would far exceed it. In the U.S. they were sports heroes, but overseas they were treated like kings.

In Portugal, 4,000 people showed up for an unannounced practice. In France, 10,000 people sat in a pouring rainstorm in an outdoor stadium; Goose Tatum played in an old-fashioned striped bathing suit, and Marques Haynes dribbled with an umbrella in one hand. In London, where basketball was known as "net ball" and considered a "sissy sport," the Globetrotters played five straight sell-outs in Wembley Stadium, one of which was broadcast nationally on British television. "No, Aunt Agatha," one British newsman enthused, "this isn't anything like the netball at your girls' school. In fact, it isn't like anything you've ever seen."

Over the next few years, South America, Asia, and Africa were added to the itinerary. Fans in those countries were even more fanatical, and Globetrotter tours became adventures of mystery and political intrigue. In Ecuador, the army had to escort the Trotters in and out of the arena, and soldiers fired tear gas canisters to prevent a mob from tearing down the walls to get in. In Brazil, a torrential downpour flooded the arena, but the promoter drilled holes in the floor to drain the water, and 14,000 fans stayed to watch. In Peru, 30,000 came to see the Trotters play in the *Plaza de Toros* bull ring. In 1951, the Trotters broke their own world attendance record, with more than 50,000 fans in a Rio soccer stadium.

Did You Know?

1895: The backboard was introduced (10 feet off the floor) to prevent fans from interfering with play (baskets were often hung off balconies).

1901: A new rule is adopted prohibiting the dribbler from shooting the ball for the 1900-01 season.

1901: First official rules published in "Basket Ball for Women" by the Spalding Athletic Library with Senda Berenson as editor. The approved women's rules are a three-court game with 5 to 10 players per side.

When the Globetrotters arrived in Japan, an estimated *two million* people lined the motorcade route to their hotel, where a four-story high poster of Goose Tatum greeted them. And in August 1959, the Trotters even penetrated the Iron Curtain, making a triumphant tour of the Soviet Union, where they were greeted by Premier Nikita Khrushchev.

Indeed, Globetrotter visits were often treated like state visits, and they played in front of numerous heads of state. In Argentina, Juan and Eva Peron were so taken with the Trotters that they invited them to their palace, and Eva decreed that "Sweet Georgia Brown" would be played at all Argentine international basketball games. In Casablanca, the Trotters played before the Sultan and his court. They gave a command performance for President Getulio Vargas of Brazil, were awarded medallions from Prince Rainier of Monte Carlo, and Crown Prince Constantine of Greece sat on the team bench. Saperstein even held a two-hour summit with Egyptian president Mohammed Naguib.

Their most celebrated command performance, however, came in 1952, when the Trotters performed for Pope Pius XII. No record player was available, so Saperstein and his entourage whistled and clapped "Sweet Georgia Brown," and the Pope's feet were tapping beneath his cassock. "My, how clever these men are," the pontiff exclaimed when it was over. "If I had not seen this with my own eyes, I would not have believed it could be done." In later years, the Globetrotters would have audiences with two other popes: John XXII and John Paul VI.

Wherever they went, the Globetrotters seemed to have a calming effect on political or labor strife. In Paris, the city's transit system was shut down by a general strike, so 8,200 people walked to the Trotters' game. During a 1956 civil war in Argentina, both sides declared a moratorium to let the Globetrotters play in Buenos Aires. In Honduras, rioting students suspended their demonstrations while the Trotters were in town. In Lima, Peru, the city was paralyzed by a violent transit strike, but the unions called off the strike for three days, until the Trotters left town.

Fact #6: The Globetrotters were used as a Cold War propaganda tool by the U.S. State Department. After witnessing the frenzied response to the Trotters in foreign countries, the State Department began a deliberate campaign to use the Trotters to counteract Soviet propaganda about the oppression of blacks in America.

The most electrifying example occurred in Berlin in August 1951, when the Globetrotters played in Olympic Stadium in Berlin, and Jesse Owens, who was working for the Globetrotters, made his first return to Berlin since his four-gold medal triumph at the 1936 Olympics.

Berlin had been a cauldron of Cold War hostilities since its partition into East and West sectors at the end of World War II. In August 1951, a communist-sponsored Third World Festival of Youth and Students was held in East Berlin, with two million young people from 50 countries in attendance. In response, West Berlin mounted its own counter-festival, and the U.S. State Department decided that the Globetrotters would be the perfect antidote to the anti-U.S. rhetoric.

With the assistance of Secretary of State Dean Acheson, the U.S. Air Force sent three C-119 "Flying Boxcars" to airlift the Globetrotters, their opposition team, and their portable basketball floor into Berlin. The State Department was hoping for 10,000 people, but at least 75,000 Germans filled the great Olympic Stadium which Adolph Hitler had built as a monument to Aryan superiority. It was the largest crowd to ever watch a basketball game, breaking the Globetrotters' previous mark (this record would stand until 2004). As one commentator noted, "The largest crowd ever to see a basketball game in the world was drawn in the former Nazi capital by a group of Negroes coached by a Jew."

At halftime, a U.S. Army helicopter landed in the middle of the field, and Owens emerged to a thunderous standing ovation. The mayor of West Berlin told Owens, "Fifteen years ago on this field, Hitler refused to offer you his hand. Now I give you both of mine."

A year later, Saperstein initiated his most ambitious promotion: an around-the-world tour spanning 33 countries and four continents. The U.S. State Department eagerly signed on as a co-sponsor, arranging stops in foreign hot spots all over the globe. As the U.S. Consul to Paraguay reported, "The visit of the Globetrotters thus pointed out a brighter picture of the Negroes' place in American life." By the time the tour ended, the Globetrotters had traveled 51,000 miles and had played before an estimated 1.5 million people.

Fact #7: The Globetrotters were the basketball equivalent of the Negro Leagues in baseball. Like their counterparts in baseball, the Globetrotters endured years of Jim Crow strictures and racial discrimination. For decades, traveling the blue highways of America, they played in backwater towns where no hotels would house them, no restaurants would feed them, and service stations wouldn't let them use the bathroom or the phone.

Even in America's biggest cities, racial prejudice followed them everywhere they went. They may have been the "Fabulous Magicians of Basketball" on the court, but once the games ended they were just like any other black men in America. Sometimes the discrimination was overt. Their team bus was set on fire one night in Indiana. In the Deep South, the Globetrotters were not allowed to play white teams, and often had to play separate games for white and black audiences. When restaurants refused to serve them, the players would say, "We're going Dutch tonight," and buy Vienna sausages and cold cuts at a local grocery to eat on the bus.

One of the many ironies in the Globetrotters' story is that they were treated better overseas than in the U.S. On the European tours, where the State Department was promoting the Trotters as exemplars of America's treatment of blacks, they were put up in four-star hotels. When they returned home, however, they were relegated to fleabag hotels in the "colored quarter" of American cities. In Cincinnati, they stayed in a dilapidated hotel with creaking stairs, broken windows, and bats flying down the halls; the players would enter their rooms armed with insect spray to kill the bedbugs. In Indianapolis, their hotel had so many cracks in the walls that the players had to sleep in their clothes to keep from freezing. Some hotels were so small that they had to sleep four players to a room, stretched out sideways across the beds. One night in Kentucky, they actually slept in a slaughterhouse, and woke up to the screams of hogs being butchered.

In Jacksonville, Florida, they were refused rooms at a nice hotel downtown, but the next morning read in the paper that "Judy the Bowling Chimpanzee" had stayed in that same hotel. As Tex Harrison, long-time Trotter player and coach, recalls, "They gave the Bowling Chimp the biggest suite and all the bananas she could eat, but they wouldn't let us stay."

Despite the racial prejudice, however, the Globetrotters played a pioneering role in breaking down racial barriers, both in sports and in American culture. The most obvious influence was in breaking the color line in the NBA. It is no coincidence that after the Globetrotters defeated the Minneapolis Lakers for the second time, in 1949, the NBA integrated the very next season. When your best team gets beaten two years in a row by the Harlem Globetrotters, who were considered a show team by many people, it's time to integrate.

In April 1950, the NBA drafted the first black players in its history, and three of the signees—Chuck Cooper, Sweetwater Clifton, and Earl Lloyd—had all been in Globetrotters' uniforms before the draft. Clifton, who played seven years with the New York Knicks, was one of the stars of the Globetrotters. Prior to being drafted, Cooper had signed a Trotter contract and had played against the College All-Stars. Lloyd had also toured with the Globetrotters after graduating from college.

Here's another irony: the Globetrotters' victories over the Lakers may have been the final wedge in breaking down the NBA's racial barriers, yet the person who stood to lose the most from that was Saperstein, who would thereafter lose his monopoly on the best black players, who increasingly signed with the NBA.

Fact #8: The Globetrotters helped keep the NBA afloat in its early years.

NBA owners begged Saperstein to play doubleheaders to draw crowds. In fact, the league might not have survived without them. "The Globetrotters meant more to the NBA than the NBA meant to the Globetrotters," Frank Deford said in the PBS documentary. "When you got the Globetrotters to come in, they meant a whole lot more to the average fan than the Sheboygan Redskins, the

Did You Know?

1903: Women's college games halves shortened from 20 to 15 minutes. Six to nine players per side are now allowed, along with 11 officials for the 1903-04 women's college season.

1906: Spalding publishes its first "Official Collegiate Basketball Guide."

Syracuse Nationals, the Fort Wayne Zollner-Pistons. Who were *they*? The Globetrotters had a name."

When the doubleheaders first began, the Trotters would play the opening game against one of their usual opposition teams, such as the Washington Generals, and NBA teams would play the "feature" game. In one famous example, on January 1, 1950, the Globetrotters played their first game ever at Madison Square Garden, on a doubleheader card with the New York Knicks and Philadelphia Warriors. Nineteen thousand fans showed up—the largest crowd to watch a professional basketball game in New York. In fact, there was a near-riot at the box office before the game, when standing room only tickets sold out in 15 minutes. About 7,000 disappointed fans were turned away. A squad of New York City cops had to be called out to calm the angry crowd. As Dick Young made clear the next morning in the *Daily News,* "Nineteen thousand fans certainly weren't there to see the Knickerbockers and Warriors."

It was obvious to NBA owners and players alike that the Globetrotters were the main attraction. "The [Globetrotters] would sell out, but they'd always play the first game," the Boston Celtics' great Bob Cousy recalled. "When they were through, half the house would get up and leave. So we knew what our position was." Eventually, the owners started asking the Trotters to play the nightcap game, just so the fans would stick around.

Those Globetrotter doubleheaders helped keep the NBA alive until the rise of the Boston Celtics' dynasty put the league on a stable footing. "I have to think that the Globetrotters' participation in those days had as much of a positive effect, in terms of selling the NBA, as anything that happened," said Cousy.

Fact #9: The Globetrotters' style of basketball had a major influence on the modern game. To put it bluntly, NBA teams today are playing Globetrotter basketball. Prior to the rise of the Globetrotters, professional basketball was a deliberate, boring repetition of chest passes around the horn and two-handed set shots. Even back in the 1930s, however, the Globetrotters were perfecting an entirely different style—a *black* style of hoops—which emphasized speed, fluidity, fast breaks, spectacular shooting, and the Globetrotters' patented weave.

That style first crossed over into "mainstream" professional ball during the brief heyday of the American Basketball Association (ABA), with its red, white, and blue basketballs and the high-flying dunks of Dr. J (Julius Erving) and Connie Hawkins. By the 1980s, it had emerged full-blown in the NBA. Think about it: Where did Magic Johnson and "Showtime" come from?

"The style that the Globetrotters had … started to pervade into the NBA game," long-time NBA coach Phil Jackson told PBS.

The Globetrotters didn't just influence basketball style, they also produced some of the greatest players in the game. These include: Inman

Jackson, the first Globetrotter showman; Sonny Boswell, a terrific outside shooter who led the team to the 1940 World Pro championship; Goose Tatum, a comic genius who invented many of the Trotters' "reams" and is considered the greatest showman of all time; Marques Haynes, who revolutionized dribbling and ball handing; Meadowlark Lemon and Curly Neal, who became international celebrities during the 1960s and '70s; and Geese Ausbie and Sweet Lou Dunbar, famous showmen from the 1980s and '90s. The Globetrotters can also claim several superstars who went on to Hall of Fame careers in the NBA, including Wilt Chamberlain, who played one year with the Trotters before going to the NBA, and returned for 11 summers to join the Trotters on the European tour. (Chamberlain always said that playing with the Trotters was the most fun he ever had in basketball.) And Connie Hawkins, who spent several years with the Trotters before going to the ABA and the NBA.

Actually, the influence of the Trotters goes even deeper. "Sweet Georgia Brown," the Magic Circle, Tatum's hook shot and Haynes' dribbling are embedded in American sports imagery, right alongside Joe DiMaggio's silky swing, Jackie Robinson's stealing home, or Joe Louis dropping Max Schmeling with a stiff right. Every kid in America who has ever picked up a basketball has tried to dribble like Marques and shoot Goose's hook. We have *all* been Globetrotters.

Fact #10: The Globetrotters are still going strong after 80 years. They nearly went bankrupt in the early 1990s, but the Globetrotters are thriving today. In fact, they're bigger than ever, playing in front of 3 million fans a year. Even in the current economic crisis, they've continued to set attendance records. And their popularity continues to expand world-wide, as they have made successful tours of China, Japan, and Australia. As basketball becomes more of a global sport, the Globetrotters remain its most visible face, truly earning their reputation as "Ambassadors of Goodwill."

As the culmination to their 80-year legacy, the Globetrotters were inducted into the Hall of Fame in 2002. Their greatest contribution to basketball, however, and their most lasting legacy, is the happiness they've brought to millions of fans. As long as we hear that whistling tune of "Sweet Georgia Brown," that joy will continue.

> The Globetrotters frequently played on **doubleheader cards** with NBA teams. 'When the Globetrotters were through, half the house would get up and leave.'
>
> — Bob Cousy

Arnold "Red" Auerbach

Arnold Auerbach:

The Man We Called Red Never Saw the World in Black and White

By Ken Dooley

His stats during his four-year career with the Boston Celtics weren't particularly impressive. He averaged 9.3 points during his rookie year and his scoring declined steadily to a low of 3.3 in his final year.

Yet Chuck Cooper has a distinction that no other black NBA player can claim, including Hall of Famers Bill Russell, KC Jones, Sam Jones, Wilt Chamberlain, Julius Erving, and Oscar Robertson.

Chuck Cooper is the man who officially integrated professional basketball when he was drafted by the Boston Celtics in April 1950. Walter Brown, then-Celtics president, made the announcement, but it was Red Auerbach who played the role of Branch Rickey, who was the general manager of the Brooklyn Dodgers when Jackie Robinson integrated major league baseball.

Auerbach had already walked away from one head coaching job because of owner interference. Brown gave him absolute control of all player decisions when Auerbach took over the last-place Celtics in 1950.

There was no national television coverage of the NBA Draft in those days. Owners and coaches met in a hotel suite where they were usually outnumbered by service personnel. Cooper's selection was not greeted enthusiastically by most of the owners. Some of them argued that letting Cooper into the NBA would destroy the financially strapped league.

Auerbach's reaction became his trademark: A long drag on a cigar and the Auerbach stare let everyone know that the decision was final. He probably had that same look when he appointed Bill Russell the first black head coach and started the first all-black team in league history.

When Auerbach sent Bill Russell, KC Jones, Sam Jones, Satch Sanders, and Willie Knaulls onto the court in 1963, it wasn't the first all-black team that he had ever seen on a basketball court.

He was 15 years old when he began to make his way into Harlem to watch the Harlem Rens, an all-black team owned and coached by Bobby Douglas. Douglas had formerly owned the Spartan Braves, a leading contender for the black national championship title every year.

The problem was that the Spartan Braves had no home court until Douglas cut a deal with William Roach, owner of the New York Renaissance Ballroom. The ballroom was in the center of Harlem, had a spacious floor, and ideal seating for basketball fans.

In return for changing the name of his team to the "New York Renaissance," Douglas was allowed to play all of his team's home games at the Renaissance. The name was shortened to the Harlem Rens, and Douglas was able to attract the best black talent in basketball.

Though racial discrimination was severe, Douglas kept his team focused. The Rens barnstormed from Boston to Kansas City and played any team – black or white – that would schedule them.

Traveling as far as 200 miles for a game, they often slept on the bus, ate cold meals, and were barred from many hotels and restaurants. Despite these obstacles, the Rens became a dominant team, winning more than 2,500 games.

The peak of their fame came in 1939 when they won the first ever World Pro Basketball Tournament, an event sponsored by the *Chicago Herald-American*. The Rens, one of only two all-black entries in the 12-team field, beat the all-white Oshkosh All Stars of the racially segregated National Basketball League (a forerunner to the NBA) in the title game.

The Rens dominated basketball for years, winning multiple Colored Basketball World Championships and routinely beating white national teams like the Original Celtics, the Philadelphia SPHAs, and the Indianapolis Kautskys.

Red Auerbach isn't the only Hall of Fame coach to admire the Harlem Rens. "To this day, I have never seen a team play better team basketball," John Wooden, the legendary college coach, once said about the Harlem Rens.

Whenever Auerbach could slip out from his father's dry cleaning store in Brooklyn, he would make his way to Harlem to watch the Rens play. He also began to attend practices, and it wasn't long before the young Auerbach caught the attention of Bobby Douglas. Auerbach never forgot how kind Douglas was in patiently answering all the questions he would throw at him.

It was the beginning of a friendship that would last for more than 40 years and influence how the game of basketball is played. The two stayed in touch during Auerbach's early career as a high school basketball coach. Douglas was one of the first to call Auerbach in 1946 when he was named the coach of the Washington Capitols for the NBA's inaugural season.

Douglas encouraged Auerbach to accept the head coaching job with the Tri-Cities Blackhawks, after things didn't work out in Washington. Auerbach was ready to walk away from basketball after he quit the Tri-Cities job because of owner Ben Kerner's interference. He sat around the house moping until Douglas called and reminded him that he "owed him for all the free admissions and coaching advice he had given over the years." He never did tell Auerbach what he expected in return.

Douglas also talked Auerbach into going to Providence to meet with Lou Pieri about taking over the Providence Steamrollers, the worst team in professional basketball. Even though Auerbach had no job or even a legitimate prospect of finding one, he leveled with Pieri and advised him to fold the franchise.

The move paid off when Walter Brown, the Celtics owner, went to Pieri for an investment in his team. Pieri agreed to invest $50,000 providing Brown interview Auerbach for the Celtics job.

Auerbach told Brown that he needed a three-year contract to take over the team. "Let me give it to you straight," Brown said. "We just finished dead last, 31 games out of first place. Lou Pieri and I just hocked our shirts and got up a quarter of a million to take the Celtics off the Garden's hands. If you don't get us moving, we'll be out of business next year, so a three-year contract doesn't mean anything. You've got one year to do the job and then we can talk — if we're both still around."

Douglas counseled Auerbach to take the job. "You'll know after a year whether you want to stay or whether they'll want you to stay," he said.

He took over the team in 1950 just prior to the NBA draft, and that's when his troubles began. The team was made up of George Kaftan, Dermie O'Connell, and Joe Mullaney, all from the College of Holy Cross. It also included Wyndol Gray and Saul Mariaschin of Harvard, Ed Leede of Dartmouth, and Tony Lavelli of Yale.

Auerbach cut them all. He also made the mistake of telling the Boston press about his feelings for "local yokels." Bob Cousy, the electrifying playmaker whose floor work brought crowds to their feet and won him first-team All-America acclaim, was about to graduate from Holy Cross.

The Boston press and fans felt that Cousy would turn the pro scene upside down with his

ball-handling magic. The problem was that Auerbach didn't share that enthusiasm, claiming that Cousy had looked out of control the few times he had seen him play. A lot of those spectacular passes bounced off teammates' heads and hands.

"All of the reporters knew more about basketball than I did and reminded their readers about it every day," Auerbach said. "We got off on the wrong foot when I refused to draft Cousy and cut all those local heroes."

Here are just a few examples of what reporters said about him in those early years:

"When he gets mad, which is a good part of the time, he glows in the dark."

"A top sergeant with corns has a better outlook on life."

"His court-side deportment at times is so bad he would be expelled from a bar brawl."

The Celtics had a lot more to overcome than bad press and a shortage of cash. Boston was a two-sport town — hockey in the winter, baseball in the summer. Brown had been a hockey man all his life, serving as president of the Boston Bruins. Auerbach knew that his biggest problem was educating the public.

"People aren't going to come to our games until they develop an appreciation and respect for

Did You Know?

1903: Under the leadership of Ralph Morgan of Pennsylvania and Harry Fisher of Columbia, 15 colleges meet in Philadelphia and New York to standardize rules and form their own governing body separate from the Amateur Athletic Union. The first set of college rules was issued the following year. The organization formed eventually evolves into the National Collegiate Athletic Association (NCAA).

what we're doing," he warned Brown. So the Celtics conducted clinics throughout their preseason exhibition.

"Teams with a few former college players and a couple of high school stars would challenge the Celtics," Auerbach said. "So we'd go out and beat them by 40 or 50 points. I wanted to sell these people on the idea that they'd never see a better basketball team than the Boston Celtics."

His public relations efforts went down in flames that first year when he drafted Charlie Share, the 6'11" giant from Bowling Green. When the word got out about the Celtics' first choice, a cry of betrayal swept across the city. Not take the Cooz (Cousy)? Had Auerbach lost his mind?

His second choice was even more controversial for NBA owners. He selected Chuck Cooper, a 6'5" guard from Duquesne. When Auerbach told Brown about his choice, he pointed out that Cooper was black.

"I don't care about the color of a ballplayer's skin," Brown answered. "He can be black, yellow, white or green if you want, as long as he can put the ball in the basket. That's the kid I want."

When Brown stood during the 1950 draft and announced that the Celtics were drafting Cooper, one of the other owners looked at him in amazement and warned, "Do you realize Cooper is a Negro?"

"I don't care if he's plaid" Brown answered. "He can play basketball."

Right after the draft, Auerbach got a call from Bobby Douglas.

"Remember when you used to come to our practices and ask me all those questions? I always listened and gave you the best answers I could. Some of my players used to kid me about spending so much time talking to this white kid from Brooklyn. I couldn't tell them why, but I can now that it's payback time.

"Red, this game of basketball is not a white man's game – it's our game. We're taller, faster, and dribble and shoot better than you guys. Our problem is not in playing the game but in *getting* to play the game.

"You just did for basketball what Branch Rickey did for baseball. So now we're even Red. Tell those Bruin fans not to worry. We're leaving hockey for you guys," Douglas promised the laughing Auerbach.

Auerbach also tried to sign Sweetwater Clifton, who was playing for the Harlem Globetrotters. Sweetwater agreed to a contract offer, but the commissioner, Maurice Podoloff, refused to approve it. Podoloff was afraid of upsetting the Globetrotters by signing their best player. A short time later, Podoloff approved a deal that let Clifton sign with the New York Knicks. The incident started a war between Podoloff and Auerbach that never ended while the commissioner was in office.

Cooper didn't have to carry the burden of being the league's only black player for very long. Clifton and Earl Lloyd joined him in 1950. Baltimore took Don Barksdale in 1951, and then came Ray Felix, Walter Dukes and Maurice Stokes. Bill Russell joined the Celtics in 1956, and then came Sam and KC Jones, Willie Naulls, Sihugo Green, Dick Ricketts, Bob Hopkins, Jim Tucker, Ed Fleming, Elgin Baylor, Guy Rodgers, and Hal Greer.

Right after that first draft, Cousy was traded to the Chicago Stags, a team that folded just before the season started. The names of their top three players – Max Zaslofsky, Andy Phillip, and Cousy – were placed in a hat and the Celtics picked out the name of Cousy.

Auerbach wasn't pleased with the draw, but he later admitted it was one of the best breaks of his coaching career. "I leveled with Bob at our first meeting," he said. "It's not just how you throw the ball in this league – whether it's a hook pass or a jump pass or a behind the back pass or a shovel pass. It's not a good pass unless a teammate catches it. You can fool the guy playing defense, but make sure you don't fool your teammates."

Cousy listened, became Rookie of the Year, and finished ninth in the league in scoring with a 15.6 average. The Celtics finished in second place, just one game behind Philadelphia. The Celtics lost to the Knicks in the playoffs, but the season represented a turnabout from the last place finish of the year before.

One of the players Auerbach passed over to select Cooper was Bill Sharman, the greatest shooter of his era. Red made up for it by trading the draft rights to Charlie Share to the Fort Wayne Pistons in exchange for Sharman and Bob Brannum. Sharman teamed with Cousy to form one of the most formidable backcourts in league history. Meanwhile, Brannum had a productive four-year career with the Celtics as a center-forward.

That move gained Auerbach the reputation of being one of the shrewdest traders in the NBA. For the next five years, the Celtics scored more points than any other team in the league, but their playoff record wasn't that good. Three times in a row, the Knicks knocked them out, and then Syracuse did the honors for the next three years.

The Celtics had all the ingredients to be a championship team except one—that big guy to get them the ball. It was a frustrating time for everyone. Brown was getting panicky because the money was running out and the Celtics still weren't taking in that much at the gate. A few times, the players had to wait for their paychecks so Brown could pay operating expenses.

Auerbach pulled a coup in the 1953 draft that eventually played a major role in getting the Celtics the big man they needed. He drafted all three of Kentucky's top stars—Frank Ramsey, Cliff Hagan, and Lou Tsioropoulos—even though each had a year of college eligibility remaining.

People first noticed Bill Russell during his junior year at San Francisco when his team won the NCAA Tournament.

They were eligible for the draft because they had been red-shirted while Kentucky sat out a one-year NCAA ban for recruiting violations. Since their original class graduated in 1953, they were eligible for the draft. Auerbach, of course, was the only one who acted on it. The league passed a rule prohibiting any such activities in the future, but Auerbach had the three guys he wanted.

The territorial draft rule was still in effect in 1956, allowing teams automatic rights to players who starred in nearby colleges, assuming their "gate appeal" would be beneficial to the league.

One of that spring's many talented graduates was Tommy Heinsohn, a strong 6'7" scoring star who had led Holy Cross to an NIT championship as a sophomore and won All-America honors in both his junior and senior seasons. Auerbach drafted Heinsohn for his scoring ability, but he knew he still needed a big man to get Celtic shooters the ball.

People first noticed Bill Russell during his junior year at San Francisco when his team won the NCAA Tournament. The Dons lost a game to UCLA early that season, and then won their next 26 in a row. The next year they went 29-0 and won the NCAA Championship again. No team had ever won 55 games without a loss, and everybody was talking about Russell.

Auerbach's old coach at George Washington, Bill Reinhart, was the first to tip him off about Russell's rebounding and defensive skills. By Russell's senior year, there were no questions about his potential as an NBA player. The problem was how were the Celtics going to get him?

Rochester had the first pick in the draft that year, but the team owner, Les Harrison, had said that Russell's demand for a $25,000 salary was too rich for his blood. St. Louis had the second choice, so Auerbach called Ben Kerner, the team owner, and got his pick for Ed MacCauley and Cliff Hagan.

Brown and Auerbach were still nervous that Harrison might change his mind and take Russell with the first pick. Brown controlled the Ice Capades at that time, and he knew that Harrison wanted to bring that show to Rochester. He offered the Ice Capades for two weeks a year in return for Harrison's pledge not to draft Russell. So the Celtics ended up getting Russell for MacCauley, Hagan, and the Ice Capades!

Not everyone shared Auerbach's conviction that Russell would succeed in the pros. He wasn't a scorer in college and some owners expressed doubt about a big man who couldn't put the ball in the basket.

Auerbach decided to put that problem to rest during his first meeting with Russell. "You're probably worried about scoring because everyone says you can't shoot well enough to play with the pros. Does that bother you?"

"Yes, I'm concerned about it," Russell answered.

"I'll make a deal with you today," Auerbach said. "I promise as long as you play here, whenever we discuss contracts we will never, ever talk about scoring or any other stats." And they never did.

Right from the beginning, Auerbach knew he had someone special in Russell. He accepted coaching from Arnie Risen, who had been around since the league started and knew a lot of the shortcuts and tricks of the big men Russell would face.

Some things just can't be taught. As the days went by, Auerbach began to detect this fierce pride Russell had and his incredible urge to win. "What made him so special…" Auerbach said. "A hundred things. Take his rebounding. He's the greatest rebounder who ever lived, and that includes Wilt Chamberlain. Chamberlain had the numbers, but in the situations where it really counted, there's never been a player who could control rebounds like Russell. Every time the ball went up in the air, Russell rebounded or boxed out or did something.

"Rebounding was only part of his genius. When he began to block shots, it was a brand new ball game. He didn't block shots the way all of the other big guys did. He would reach underneath the ball or on its side if he had to. Most shot-blockers are what I call shot-swatters, like Chamberlain was. They hit the ball any way they can, and it sails out of bounds or it bounces on the floor where anybody who reaches it first can pick it up.

"Russell made shot-blocking an art. He would pop the ball straight up and grab it like a rebound or else redirect it into the hands of one of his teammates. You never saw Russell bat a ball into the third balcony the way those other guys did. When Russell blocked a shot he not only took the potential basket away from the other team, but kept the ball for his own team.

> The **difference** between Bill Russell and Wilt Chamberlain can be summed up in two sentences. Bill Russell joined the team. The team joined Wilt Chamberlain
>
> — Red Auerbach

"The difference between Bill Russell and Wilt Chamberlain can be summed up in two sentences. Bill Russell joined the team. The team joined Wilt Chamberlain."

The Celtics won their first NBA championship in 1957, and went on to win 11 of the next 13 championships.

While blacks had come of age in basketball, some owners worried about the effect they would have on the gate. There was a period of years when some of the owners decided they would have no more than two blacks, then three, then four, then five. It wasn't anything that anyone talked about, it just happened.

Auerbach and Brown never bought into that thinking. Brown told off more than one Boston reporter for warning him that ticket sales might dwindle if the Celtics kept adding black players. At one league meeting, Commissioner Podoloff warned that blacks seemed to be dominating the sport and he suggested that owners consider a quota system.

Brown jumped out of his chair and said he didn't care how many black players were in the NBA or how many were coming in. He said he wouldn't accept a quota system and would sell the team before doing so. That's about as far as the discussion went and it never came up again. The notion that fans would shy away as more black players entered the league has been demolished by attendance figures.

While blacks faced no restrictions on the basketball courts, there were still many closed doors in the cities where they played. In 1961, the Celtics played an exhibition game in Wichita, Kansas. When they got to a hotel, Sam Jones and Tom Sanders went into a coffee shop. A waitress came over and said, "We don't serve colored here."

When Russell heard about it, he called the airport to find the next flight to New York, Boston or Chicago. KC Jones joined Russell, Sam Jones, and Satch Sanders, so the Celtics were about to lose four key team members.

Auerbach argued that the waitress had made a mistake, but the 10,000 people who were coming to see them play shouldn't be penalized. "Why not go out there and show them you're bigger than some waitress in a lousy hotel?" When Auerbach couldn't budge them, he tried another tack.

"I'll call the manager of the hotel and we'll all go down right now and eat as a team," Auerbach promised. "I don't want to eat as a team," Sam Jones objected. "I want to eat as a person."

Auerbach put his black players on a flight to Boston and played with an all-white team that got thrashed. When Auerbach called Brown and told him what had happened, Brown was furious. "You shouldn't have played that game," Brown said. "You should have left with the whole team."

 "We had to play to get our expenses back," Auerbach argued.

"The hell with the expenses," Brown screamed at Auerbach. "They didn't deserve the game after what they did to our kids."

The Celtics had another incident when they played an exhibition in Marion, Indiana. The mayor threw a luncheon before the game and gave the players miniature keys to the city. Everything went down hill after the game. Russell, Sam and KC Jones, Sanders, Carl Braun, and Gary Phillips decided to eat at a local cocktail lounge.

There were at least a dozen empty tables when they got there, but they were told they couldn't be seated without reservations. Russell called the mayor, and he promised to deal with the owner of the club the next day. They all met in the mayor's office but nothing was done to the club owner after he explained that all of the empty tables were "reserved." Sam Jones summed it up best when he said. "They gave us the keys to the city, but it didn't open any doors."

The Celtics had another incident in Charlotte, North Carolina, when they played a league game against Minneapolis. Auerbach didn't anticipate any problems because the NCAA regionals had played there the previous year and blacks were allowed to stay and eat in the same hotel.

He was wrong. Russell was sent to a fleabag hotel with a bed about half his size. Sam Jones had to stay with a fraternity brother and KC Jones and Ben Swain went to a motel.

Russell wanted to leave, but Auerbach used the argument that he knew something about prejudice because he was a minority, too. "I know you're Jewish," Russell said. "But your face is white." Auerbach didn't have any comeback for that but everyone agreed to play because it was a regular season game. The Celtics won but it came at a terrible expense, Auerbach admitted more than 40 years later.

"I know that Russell and some of the other players had reservations about my actions when they were treated so poorly. I took the position then that my players owed it to themselves to stay and play and let the fans see how great they were.

"I guess I thought this would help knock the barriers down a little faster. Walter Brown said I should have taken the team out of those towns and told everybody down there that they didn't deserve to have men like that in their midst. Now, when I look back, I think that Walter was right."

Auerbach didn't make many other mistakes, retiring as one of the greatest evaluators of talent the game has ever known. With the last pick in the draft in 1962, he selected John Havlicek who provided the spark off the bench during the Celtics' dynasty years of the 1960s. During the 1970s, Havlicek was the trusted veteran who captained youthful teams to championships in 1974 and 1976.

Auerbach drafted the three stars at the University of Kentucky because of an eligibility technicality. He drafted Larry Bird in his junior year, the only executive who realized that Bird was eligible because his class had graduated.

He traded Charlie Share for Bob Brannum and Bill Sharman. In his 11-year NBA career, Sharman was voted to the All-NBA first or second team seven times and played in eight NBA All-Star games. He got Russell, one of the greatest players in the history of the NBA, in a trade for players (and the Ice Capades). He traded Bob McAdoo to the Detroit Pistons for M.L. Carr and draft choices that became Robert Parish (through a trade) and Kevin McHale.

He traded Gerald Henderson for a draft pick that he turned into Lenny Bias, the All-America from the University of Maryland. Lenny died of a drug overdose before playing a single game with the Celtics, a tragedy that Auerbach never got over.

He always preferred picking his own talent and training them in the "Celtic" way. From the day a player joined the Celtics, he understood that discipline was a very big thing. There were no loudmouths, no complainers, no dissenters, and no clubhouse lawyers like on other teams.

Auerbach told the players that he wasn't worried about keeping them happy. "There are 12 of you and only one of me so it's a lot easier for you to study me and find ways to keep me happy." He never expected his players to love him. He just wanted them to respect him and his coaching decisions.

It wasn't any accident that the Celtics had a dress code when they traveled as a team – shirts, ties, and jackets were mandatory. Every time out, Auerbach inspected his team to make sure there were no shirttails hanging out, no uniform straps twisted and turned. It was all part of the Celtic image. His team looked crisp and confident. Regardless of how they felt inside, they always looked like winners.

He even had certain rules for huddles that gave his team a psychological edge. No Celtic ever sat down during a time-out. He wanted to show contempt for the other team. *They* had to sit down. *They* were tired. *They* needed rest. But the Celtics were not tired. The Celtics did not need rest. They were always ready to run back out there and chase the other team off the court.

He wanted the other team to look at the Celtics and see how strong, fresh, and confident they were. He wanted it to bother them, distract them, embarrass them. He never went along with the famous line from the Grantland Rice poem: "It matters not that you won or lost, but how you played the game."

His competitive strategy can be summed up in a few sentences. "It is important whether you win or lose. Being a sore loser is not a bad thing. Only losers accept losing. Who says you can't build character when you win? As long as you're going to keep score, you've got to go out there with the idea of winning."

His search for a competitive edge gave him the idea for the "sixth man" concept. One year he took a look at his starting five and decided they could hold their own with any other team. The problem was that two or three other NBA coaches could make the same claim.

All around the league, everybody started their best players. "Suppose I don't start my best?" Auerbach asked himself. "Suppose I start 80% of my best. Now after five, six or seven minutes go by, it's time to substitute. Their 100% is getting tired and so is my 80%. In goes their sub and in goes my sixth man. What happens? They've decreased their proficiency while I've increased mine."

It wasn't long before other teams started holding out a starter in response to the Celtics' strategy. But Auerbach still had the edge. "I've got them. I'm controlling the tempo, the play. They're following me. I'm in their heads."

He never had much use for Xs and Os and all kinds of fancy diagrams that coaches now use during games. He never believed in gadgets or gimmicks. In all his years of coaching, the Celtics had just six plays with options.

"If you have too many plays, too many picks, too many intricacies in each play, the execution will suffer. Keep it simple. That was my rule. You have one move away from the ball, a little pick, pop up a shot, very simple. We only used plays if our fast break didn't work or we were playing for the last shot of the period. The fast break was the key to Celtic basketball."

He always preached that a play didn't have to succeed to be good. It might be good just because it opens up something else. "We never forced plays. If one didn't work, we tried something else. The play is merely a beginning. If it works, great. If not, go on to something else."

Lee Iacocca was chairman of Chrysler when he wrote these words in an introduction to *MBA: Management by Auerbach*:

"Red, like me, is the son of immigrants, and one who didn't stay in the family business. It took him seven years to win a title. That wasn't the amazing thing, at least to me. The amazing thing was that he could keep doing it fifteen more times. The way he did it is one of the key lessons of his life. He worked people hard and then convinced them they were good. They began to believe it. They call it 'Celtics Pride.' I call it great motivation from the most successful basketball coach of all time."

Auerbach's competitive philosophy can be summed up in a message he delivered to his team every year: "It's not enough to be good if you have the ability to be better. It's not enough to be good if you can be great."

He always had great answers to questions about his team or the league. One frequent question he got in later years was, "Who was the better basketball player – Bill Russell or Larry Bird?" He would always say that Russell was the greatest player he ever coached. Then he would pause and add, "Of course, I never coached Larry Bird."

He never dodged questions about his team or the game of basketball. He wasn't always comfortable with off-the-court subjects, especially with what he called "this black and white thing." When Boston was undergoing all of the problems associated with bussing and public school integration, city officials wanted him to step in and become a voice for moderation.

He turned them down flatly, not because he didn't care, but because he considered himself to be a basketball coach, not a politician or an agent for social change. He bristles when people suggest that he was a social activist in knocking down the barriers to black players in the NBA.

He drafted Cooper because of his basketball skills, not the color of his skin. He started five black players because they represented the best team he could put on the floor, with Havlicek coming in as the sixth man. He appointed Russell the first black player-coach because he was the best man for the job. He pushed to have Bobby Douglas admitted to the Basketball Hall of Fame because he belonged there.

The color of a person's skin never influenced him one way or the other. He never really understood why it should matter to anyone else.

A Shot for the Ages

By Blair Kerkhoff

Early in his career, sometime between the gravity-defying air-walking shoe commercial and his first NBA championship ring, Michael Jordan admitted not knowing much about basketball's history. But when told of the player widely credited with being the first to lift his feet off the ground and shoot the ball one-handed—the jump shot's originator—Jordan wanted to hear more.

He was told the story of Hank Luisetti.

College basketball's timeline is dotted with transcendent players. George Mikan and Bob Kurland were the game's first great centers and individual rivals. Bill Russell was the first great winner, Wilt Chamberlain and Lew Alcindor (later Kareem Abdul-Jabbar) changed the rules. Jerry Lucas, Elgin Baylor, Oscar Robertson, Pete Maravich, Bill Walton, David Thompson, Magic Johnson, Larry Bird, Patrick Ewing, and others all delivered new standards of excellence.

But the first to make a profound statement of change was Luisetti, the 6'2" Stanford star of the 1930s.

"He revolutionized shooting with his jumper," said Coach Mike Montgomery, formerly of Stanford. "Somebody would have come up with it somewhere along the line, but he was the first guy to have tremendous success with it, and it had a major impact on basketball."

Through the game's Naismith period—from the time James invented basketball in 1891 until he died in 1939—offensive basketball was a mostly patterned affair. Passes, passes, and more passes before a shot attempt were the norm as games plodded along.

After made baskets—and there weren't many—the game returned to center court for a jump ball. The shot clock was decades away. Scores rarely exceeded 50. Individual 20-point games were considered extraordinary.

They started playing something entirely different at Stanford soon after Luisetti enrolled in 1934, and when he played on the varsity a year later word started to spread of this team that liked to run and a player who could score at will.

In 1935, Stanford opened Luisetti's sophomore season by scoring unheard of totals of 71 and 73 points in its first two games. The Indians had topped 50 once in the previous five years.

> Stanford's Hank Luisetti changed the game forever ... he **jumped** as he shot.

Stanford won a school-record 21 games, averaged 49.2 points—10 more than it had scored in any other year—and Luisetti averaged 14 points, a freakish number for the day. This style, so entertaining and successful, made perfect sense to Luisetti, his teammates and Coach John Bunn.

But it would take two games, one in each of the next two seasons, for basketball to become convinced of its future.

The first was played on December 30, 1936, when 17,632 packed Madison Square Garden in New York for the evening's doubleheader. Georgetown defeated New York University in the opener but the game had a distinct undercard feel.

The main attraction matched mighty Long Island University, riding a 43-game winning streak, against Stanford, the unconventional West Coast squad that, according to New York City sportswriters, would get exposed on the grand stage.

And the media was stoked for this one. A college basketball game had never received this much publicity. A few days earlier, New York writers had traveled to Philadelphia to catch Stanford and Luisetti defeat Temple, the second-best team in the East.

Still, the sassy scribes weren't convinced. Coach Clair Bee's Long Island team was the nation's best. The Blackbirds had won their 10 games that season by an average of 28 points and in 6'8" center Art Hillhouse, they had size no opponent could match.

And even though most of Stanford's starting five were from San Francisco, like Luisetti, or Los Angeles, none had experienced anything like this.

When the lights dimmed just before the game, Stanford center Art Stoefen panned the building now reduced to a smoky haze and saw thousands of small lights, like fireflies. Only the lights weren't moving. They were the fans' cigarettes, rising three levels above the court.

It was true, Stoefen later said, Stanford was overwhelmed by the atmosphere in the early going. But they found comfort in watching Long Island, conducting warm-ups in the prevalent style of the day, taking shots with their feet planted, heels together and two hands pushing the ball toward the basket.

Luisetti chuckled to himself. He knew defending the two-handed set shot was like guarding a statue.

The game was tight early, 11-11 midway through the first half. But Long Island sensed trouble. The team had never seen an opponent play like this. Defensively, when man-to-man was the accepted practice, Stanford used a zone and the team's quickness allowed it to quickly cover LIU shooters.

The Blackbirds soon learned they had no answer for Stanford's unorthodox style on offense and defense and the Indians ran to a 22-14 halftime lead. In the second half, they held LIU scoreless for seven minutes and ran away with a 45-31 victory.

Luisetti showed more passing than shooting skills on this night and still finished with 15 points. He changed directions by dribbling behind his back. He threw behind the back passes, a style Bob Cousy would popularize first with Holy Cross and later with the Celtics.

And the few shots Luisetti took were watched with awe. The Garden crowd had not seen anything like this. He would dribble around a defender, stop, elevate, and release it with one hand. Luisetti was playing a grainy black-and-white game in hi-def.

Stanford received a standing ovation as it left the court, and the New York writers were convinced they had seen the future. *The New York Post's* Stanley Frank put it like this:

"Overnight, and with a suddenness as startling as Stanford's unorthodox tactics, it had become apparent today that New York's fundamental concept of basketball will have to be radically changed if the metropolitan district is to remain among the progressive centers of court culture in this country. Every one of the amiable clean-cut Coast kids fired away with leaping one-handed shots which were impossible to stop."

But not everybody was convinced.

"That's not basketball," said Nat Holman of City College of New York. "If my boys ever shot one-handed I'd quit coaching."

Holman had to change his philosophy. Two years after the benchmark game, every hoopster entering a New York college was shooting the ball one-handed.

Angelo Luisetti was born in 1916 to Italian immigrant parents near the North Beach section of San Francisco. His father, Steven, was a cook and eventually opened his own restaurant. Hank was an only child who wore braces as a child to strengthen bowed legs.

The nearby playground had a basketball goal, and even as a boy, Luisetti would sling the ball

> **If my boys ever shot one-handed, I'd quit coaching.**
>
> — Nat Holman, CCNY

toward the basket with one hand, almost like a discus.

In interviews before he died in 2002 at age 86, Luisetti said his one-handed shot developed out of necessity.

"Shooting two-handed, I just couldn't reach the basket," Luisetti said. "I'd get the ball, take a dribble or two and jump and shoot on the way up. I'd let the ball go right near my face. I'd push and shoot, off my fingertips.

"I was lucky with my coaches in high school and college. Because I made the baskets, they left me alone and didn't try to change my shot."

Luisetti's high school, Galileo of San Francisco, won two city championships, which earned him a scholarship to Stanford.

There, he played for Bunn, who had been well-schooled in basketball's fundamentals. He played and coached at Kansas and was the program's first assistant under Phog Allen. From 1921-30, Bunn coached the freshmen team and played the same deliberate style as Allen's varsity team, which won six straight Missouri Valley championships in the 1920s.

That was the game Bunn brought to Stanford without much success. The Indians posted losing records in Bunn's first five years and his record of 41-70 entering the 1935-36 season did not portend a long future on the sideline.

Luisetti's arrival changed Bunn's approach. The coach, who took physical education classes at Kansas under Dr. James Naismith, took an important lesson from the game's inventor that he applied at Stanford. Basketball should be fun. Naismith wasn't even convinced basketball should be coached. It's about kids on a court having fun.

That idea struck Bunn when he observed Luisetti pile up points and pass the ball like a magician. In one of the greatest philosophical adjustments in coaching history, Bunn turned his team loose. Bunn said in 1938 that "Hank Luisetti is the young man who made a coach out of John Bunn. He'd make a coach out of anybody."

But Luisetti also credited Bunn for not changing his shooting style or approach to the game. The Indians finished 1937 with a 25-2 record and were recognized by the Helms Foundation as the national champion. Luisetti's junior season would be Stanford's best as a team. But his best game - the best by any individual to date - would come in his senior year.

Luisetti never considered himself a scorer. He could shoot like nobody else but he always believed play-making was his greatest strength.

On New Year's Day, 1938, his teammates had had enough of Luisetti's unselfishness. They wanted him to make scoring history.

The Indians were working their way back to California and had taken out Holman's CCNY and Long Island in New York. After a loss at Temple, Stanford hopped a train to Cleveland where it would meet Duquesne.

On this night, nearly every time Luisetti passed the ball he got it back. Teammates insisted that he shoot and Luisetti scored like nobody else ever had in a game. In a 92-27 victory, Luisetti tossed in running one-handers from every angle, mostly from 15 to 18 feet, and amassed a college record 50 points on 23 field goals and four free throws.

Luisetti was almost apologetic. In a post-game interview he told a reporter that he wasn't trying to break records and that it wasn't fair to run up the score.

Bunn said his decision to leave Luisetti in for as long as he did was influenced by the atmosphere and a crowd that cheered wildly for the star.

"I couldn't take him out, it wouldn't have been fair to the crowd," Bunn said. "Even the boys on the bench argued when I made a break to send in a replacement."

In his biography *The Game Changer: How Hank Luisetti Revolutionized America's Great Indoor Game*, author Philip Pallette said Luisetti needed a police escort to leave the building because fans tore at his clothes.

In Luisetti's senior year, Stanford finished 21-3 and posted its third straight 20-victory season. He was named national player of the year and an All-America for the third straight season. His 19.3 scoring average topped the nation, and it was believed his 1,596 career points were a national record.

But that total, often cited in basketball record books, rolled in his freshman team numbers, and those don't count in NCAA statistics. Luisetti finished with 1,291 career points and a 16.1

career average, still amazing numbers for his era. The 50-point game remained a school record through the 2008-09 season as well.

No statistics were kept for assists or steals or undoubtedly Luisetti would have ranked high in those season and career categories.

His opportunity for more widespread attention was damaged by unfortunate timing.

Stanford won its final 14 games in 1938, but after beating Oregon twice in a best-of-three series to determine the Pacific Coast Conference title, the season was over. The NCAA Tournament didn't begin until 1939, with Oregon becoming the first national champion.

That inaugural tournament was a financial bust and nearly went out of business. How much momentum would have been realized had Luisetti been the first NCAA Tournament star?

Three years later, Stanford won an NCAA title of its own, defeating Dartmouth for the championship in Kansas City, and although Luisetti had moved on, his influence was still felt.

Bill Cowden, a member of that team, remembered how the Indians all shot like Luisetti, jumping one-handers, and Darmouth was a set-shooting team. Stanford won in a rout.

Plus, there is scant evidence of Luisetti's game preserved in newsreel. Newspaper clippings and word of mouth had to suffice. Still, some 13 years after completing his college career, Luisetti was recognized by the Associated Press as the second greatest basketball player in the first half of the 20th century after George Mikan, and in 1959 he was elected as an original member of the Naismith Memorial Basketball Hall of Fame.

Some historical clarity is in order.

Basketball researchers have found players before Luisetti who shot jumpers and with one hand.

In his book, *The Origins of the Jump Shot*, John Christgau credits eight pioneers throughout the nation who developed the modern day jump shot and Luisetti isn't listed among them.

Kenny Sailors, who helped Wyoming win the 1943 national championship, had a more modern-looking jump shot. "I played against Hank Luisetti in an AAU tournament in the '40s," Sailors said. "He had a running one-hander. It was a great shot. But he didn't stop and jump like I did."

Joe Fulks, who starred with the Philadelphia Warriors and once held the NBA single-game scoring record with 63 points, also is recognized as a jump-shooting originator.

Other historians are adamant about including Luisetti on any list of jump shooting pioneers.

What Luisetti had that the others didn't was a Madison Square Garden moment that some sports historians have called college basketball's version of the Baltimore Colts-New York Giants 1958 "greatest game ever played" in pro football.

Luisetti never got caught up in such talk. He lived a rich life after Stanford, although basketball was part of it for only a few more years, and never professionally.

But he did cash in on his hoop fame. In 1938, he received top billing along with Bette Grable in the movie "Campus Confession." The poster reads, "A peppy college romance! A real basketball game!"

The flick bombed, and worse, Luisetti was suspended from the Amateur Athletic Union for one year because he was paid $10,000 for his role and was filmed playing basketball.

The suspension was lifted for the 1940-41 season and he helped the San Francisco Olympic Club to the finals of the national AAU Tournament.

His best post-college season came in 1943-44, playing for a Navy team, St. Mary's Pre-Flight. But soon after the season he developed spinal meningitis, and despite receiving offers from professional basketball teams after the war, he never played again.

After Luisetti coached his company's AAU team, Stewart Chevrolet, to the 1951 championship, he was through with basketball. He entered the travel business and retired in 1985.

Three years later, Stanford erected a bronze statue inside its basketball arena of Luisetti in his classic shooting pose. A former teammate, Phil Zonne, was the artist who worked without a fee and captured Luisetti extending his right arm and the ball leaving the tips of his fingers.

A shot for the ages.

Geno Auriemma and the UConn Huskies understand what it takes to be perfect.

Perfect Is Barely Good Enough

By Jackie MacMullan

There had been five previous championships, each of them distinct, all of them defined by the personalities of the women who shaped Connecticut's program. Their coach, Geno Auriemma, once likened his title teams to his children. While they sprang from shared roots, similar philosophies and a singular vow of commitment, their paths to greatness were invariably divergent.

And yet, whenever his University of Connecticut women's teams were crowned champions, Auriemma was able to trace a single thread that connected them - a sense that the requisite chemistry and focus had already been firmly established before they played a single game.

That uniform component occurred to him in the summer of 2008 as he reclined in his beach chair, his toes encased in sand, his eyes fixed on the horizon. It was early July, and for the moment the whir of the college basketball treadmill had subsided. As Auriemma studied the waves cresting along the Jersey shore, he considered the possibilities for his returning Connecticut basketball team. The previous spring his team had advanced to the NCAA Final Four but was unceremoniously dismissed by a superior Stanford club.

It had been more than four years since Connecticut had won it all. The program had reached such lofty standards that this "drought" had actually proved to be cause for alarm in the local community. Even Auriemma and his staff found themselves pondering whether their approach to recruiting, training, and coaching needed to be tweaked. Were they working hard enough? Had they lost their edge?

Never mind the fact that Auriemma already owned two of the eleven perfect seasons in modern college basketball and the coaches of all those teams were of course enshrined in the same Hall of Fame as him. He knew the fans demanded more. In fact, he himself demanded more.

The Huskies had just landed one of their best recruiting classes ever, yet in a bizarre twist the nation's top-rated player, Elena Delle Donne, abruptly withdrew from Connecticut after just a few days on campus.

Delle Donne was a can't-miss prospect who skipped her high school graduation to enroll in summer school at Connecticut and was on course to align herself as the next great link in the Huskies lineage of top-flight talent.

Instead, citing burnout and homesickness, she left campus and retreated to her native Delaware.

For most programs, the unexpected loss would have been a staggering blow.

Yet lounging on the beach more than a month after Delle Donne's shocking decision, Auriemma, the architect of five championships and two undefeated seasons, the self-admitted chronic worrier who saw the glass as neither half full nor half empty but *completely* empty, couldn't contain his glee.

"We've got a chance," Auriemma informed the seagulls flying overhead. "We could win it all."

His next thought was so tantalizing, yet so taboo, he didn't dare share it even with the birds. Auriemma never said it aloud, but the thought most definitely occurred to him: it was entirely possible his 2008-09 Huskies could go undefeated.

The groundwork for his optimism had been laid when his team arrived back at Gampel

Pavilion in the wee hours of the morning after its Final Four loss to Stanford. The Huskies were disappointed and weary, but Auriemma summoned his returning players into the locker room and individually and systematically exposed their shortcomings. The players accepted the criticism stoically. They didn't need their coach to highlight their failures; they already had committed them to memory.

Auriemma informed them he would not designate a day for their offseason program to begin. Normally the staff gave the players a week or so to recover, but this time it was up to his team.

Three days later, the Huskies were at his door.

"We're ready, Coach," Maya Moore informed him. "Let's go."

Moore had been named an All-America as a freshman. She was an exceptional catch-and-shoot player whose quickness also made her a threat driving to the basket. Her scoring repertoire, in addition to her innate defensive abilities, was enhanced by her unflagging work ethic and her natural leadership skills. Moore's poise prompted Auriemma to liken her to Derek Jeter, the New York Yankees shortstop who embodied the great tradition of the pinstripes. Her freshman sea-

son had been so prolific his only concern was how she could possibly top it.

Center Tina Charles was another matter. She was a gifted low post player with tremendous rebounding and shot-blocking skills who came from the famed Christ the King High School in New York City. Although Charles had nearly averaged a double-double (14.2 points, 9.2 rebounds) in her sophomore season, Auriemma expressed his disappointment that she had "settled" for good play instead of great play. He would ride his center harder than any other player throughout the course of the 2008-09 season because he knew his team could only go as far as the congenial Charles was willing to take them.

There were no motivational tactics required for his floor leader, senior point guard Renee Montgomery, a 5'7" whirling dervish who was the only player in Connecticut's illustrious history to rank in the top 10 in points, assists, steals and 3-pointers. Yet those numbers were a hollow consolation for a fiercely competitive player who was in her final season and still hadn't won an NCAA title.

Just weeks before the season began, Auriemma waved Montgomery into his office and shut the door. He ran a highlight reel of Phoenix Suns point guard Steve Nash, a two-time NBA Most Valuable Player who made

his mark by controlling the tempo of the basketball game.

Nash thrived as both a scorer and a facilitator, and as Montgomery watched him force the game's action on film, she turned to Auriemma and said, "Coach, I'd *love* to play that way."

"Then let's do it," he responded.

And so Connecticut re-invented itself as a cadre of gunslingers. The first championship team in 1995 achieved a perfect 35-0 mark by adhering to the disciplines of the triangle offense, which required precision passing, cutting and infinite patience, qualities embodied by their star, Rebecca Lobo.

That playbook was scrapped with Montgomery at the controls. Now it was shoot first and pass later. The first time Montgomery streaked down the court and pulled up for a jumper just seconds into the game, a few of the faithful Connecticut fans actually gasped. Montgomery and Moore continuously pushed tempo and fired off shots before the opposing teams had a chance to set their defense. The more frenetic the pace, the more the players thrived.

Montgomery prepared for that pace by arranging for pick-up games over the summer with members of the Connecticut football team. The exercise was cordial until the football players began dunking on their heads. It was then that Montgomery kicked into overdrive, admonishing her teammates if they showed even the slightest hint of intimidation.

Moore's approach proved to be more measured. She was a student of the game who was conservative by nature, a trait that came to light during the team's preseason retreat. One of the exercises the players were required to complete was to navigate a walk through the woods while blindfolded, holding onto to teammates both in front and behind. While a number of the Huskies plunged along in the darkness with little regard to what was ahead, Moore was notably cautious, often traversing obstacles backwards rather than risk falling on her face.

It was a revelation to Auriemma to witness his star player proceed so carefully. It was a complete departure from his previous superstar, Diana Taurasi, who won three championships with guts and bravado and very little planning. Once, when she stole a pass then pulled up for a three-pointer on a 1-on-3 fast break, an infuriated Auriemma screeched, "Dee, do you ever think before you do anything?"

Taurasi shrugged. The shot had gone in.

As the 2008-09 season drew near, Auriemma realized he needed to prod Moore into being a little more spontaneous. "I'm not saying I want her to be as spontaneous as Dee," he mused. "Somewhere in between the two of them lies the greatest player ever to walk the earth."

Moore didn't require her coach to outline what would make her a better player. She needed to add a little swagger, to take the ball off the dribble more, to create more free throw opportunities for herself. She needed to impose her will on the game more consistently.

No one had won four championships in four years at Connecticut, and while that milestone had already slipped from Moore's grasp, her mantra quickly became, "It's national championship or bust."

"If you play at Connecticut," she explained, "why would you have any other goal than to win it all?"

The team's preseason practices were so intense and hotly contested, Connecticut soon craved competition other than themselves. When the Huskies finally played Georgia Tech in their opener on November 17, they had worked themselves into such a "championship" frenzy they were playing not to lose instead of playing to win. The score was tied 34-34 at halftime and late in the second half, on the strength of three-point shooting, Georgia Tech still remained within three, 65-62.

A suffocating man-to-man and some timely baskets by Charles put the game away in the final minutes, but after the 11-point victory, the Huskies trudged to their locker room as though they had lost.

"My fault," their coach told them. "I got you too hyped up. Just play. Let's have fun and play."

Thirteen days later when Connecticut matched up against No. 4 Oklahoma and its All-America

center Courtney Paris, the mindset had clearly shifted. Charles held Paris scoreless in the first half (she would finish with 14 for the game) and joined Moore and Montgomery in posting a double-double. The stunning 106-78 Connecticut win on national television prompted Montgomery to declare, "You know, we've got something special going on here."

The contributions in the Oklahoma win were not limited to UConn's celebrated trio. Freshman Caroline Doty finished a perfect 6-for-6 from behind the 3-point line and had settled in as an integral part of the starting line-up.

Doty was on her way to another productive shooting night (5-for-11 in three's) on January 17 when she tore her anterior cruciate ligament in her knee and was lost for the season. Almost immediately the euphoria of a gaudy 54-point win over Syracuse faded. Doty's injury was the one low point in an otherwise storybook season. The Huskies had exactly 24 hours to get over it and prepare for North Carolina on January 19.

Connecticut came in ranked No. 1 and the Tar Heels ranked No. 2, with both teams undefeated and North Carolina riding a 31-game winning streak at Chapel Hill.

It was what the Huskies liked to call "a statement game." Connecticut held UNC to 30 percent shooting and hoisted 39 three-pointers. They led 46-30 at halftime and won by 30 points. Sophomore Lorin Dixon, who (temporarily) replaced Doty in the starting line-up, was a perfect 5-for-5 from the floor, while Moore posted 40 points and 13 rebounds.

> # If you play at Connecticut, why would you have any other goal than to win it all?
>
> — Maya Moore

The bulls-eye on Connecticut's back had grown exponentially, and talk began in earnest of an undefeated season and a sixth undisputed championship.

Auriemma, who had expertly steered dominant teams before, understood the trappings of complacency, so he turned up the heat on his players. While the outside world viewed the wins of staggering margins as a cakewalk, it was, in fact, grueling by design.

His players came to realize Auriemma did not coach the same way in October as he did in March. From the start of the season until the end of February he was impossible to please, a perfectionist who would ferret out the one flaw in an otherwise impressive performance, then harp on it and pick at it like a scab that was never allowed to heal.

During their remarkable 2008-09 season, he routinely took a game the Huskies had won by 30 points and broke it down into a 10-minute clip that gave the appearance of a team that had lost by 20. He harped on footwork, proper cuts, denial defense, boxing out. Every dribble, every pass and every shot was subjected to stifling scrutiny. He did it to prepare them mentally for the rigors of March, when one loss meant the season was over.

No one bore the brunt of Auriemma's barbs more than Charles. Midway through a routine win over Rutgers on February 3, the coach yanked his starting center from the line-up after just 14 minutes of what he determined to be lackluster play. After the team's victory, he bellowed, "How does it feel to know we won that game without you?"

He banned her from the next team practice. Charles texted him asking Auriemma to re-consider; when he didn't, she sat watching the swim team practice and wept. She was a reluctant star, content to play well and help the team win. Her coach was demanding more, and on that bitter New England February day, she wasn't sure she could deliver it.

Two weeks later, Charles and her teammates found themselves in some unfamiliar territory against Notre Dame. The Fighting Irish jumped out to a 6-0 lead and actually led for 16 minutes and 53 seconds, the longest stretch a team had the upper hand on the Huskies all season. The advantage was no fluke. Notre Dame's defense held Connecticut to 31 percent shooting in the first half and scorer Lindsay Schrader proved to be a difficult match-up.

Though they only led 36-33 at the half, there was no sense of panic in the Huskies locker room. "We knew how it to fix it," Moore explained. "As long as we played our game we were going to be fine."

Connecticut used a crushing 22-1 run in the second half to regain control of the game. The final score was 76-66. It was the closest anyone would come during the entire season.

After finishing the regular season with a 30-0 mark, the Huskies went on to crush Louisville in the Big East Conference Championship. In the NCAA tournament, they beat Vermont by 39 points, Florida by 29, California by 24 and Arizona State by 19.

Cal earned the distinction of building an 8-point lead in the first half by doing an admirable job on the glass against women's basketball Goliath. But like so many challengers before them, the Golden Bears couldn't withstand the lethal combination of lockdown defense and precision offense.

Connecticut's leading scorer that day was freshman guard Tiffany Hayes (her signing was overlooked during the Delle Donne hype), who had quietly worked her way into the starting line-up in early February. She torched Cal for 28 points on 9-for-10 shooting.

By the time Connecticut advanced to the Final Four, they were beating teams by an average of 31.1 points.

Their rematch with Stanford in the national semi-final proved to be anti-climactic; Montgomery had 26 points, 6 assists, and 4 steals and the Huskies prevailed in an 83-64 rout.

That left only Louisville in the way of an unbeaten national championship season. Connecticut had already easily dispatched of Louisville twice during the season, but Auriemma fretted it would be challenging to beat the same team three times in a row. He challenged Charles to play up to her capabilities. "I want you to go out and prove you are the best center in the country," he said.

She happily obliged, shredding Louisville for 25 points (on 11-for-13 shooting) and 19 rebounds. With the 76-54 victory, Connecticut had claimed five of the nine championships of the decade. The 2009 champions became the first team in NCAA Division I history (men or women) to go an entire season undefeated by winning games by 10 or more points. It was a dominating body of work by a group of young women whose focus rarely wavered.

It has been a fascinating basketball journey for Auriemma, who arrived in Storrs, Connecticut, in 1985 to a field house with a leaky roof, a tiny locker room shared with the softball team and hopelessly outdated uniforms. Back then, losing was expected, and accepted.

Now, only a championship will do.

The Connecticut women—and their coach— wouldn't have it any other way.

Basketball Blueprint: How the 1992 Dream Team Changed the Game Around the Globe

By Jack McCallum

The idea seemed counter-intuitive, screwy even, when it first started to make the rounds in the late 1980s. It was:

Invite NBA players to participate for the United States in the Olympics, watch them sweep through the tournament like Sherman through Atlanta, then sit back and see the game start to improve as a result of the routs.

Huh?

But that was the idea that began to circulate around the halls of FIBA, the organization that ran (still runs) the international game. FIBA's executive director, the Serbian-born Boris Stankovic, an enthusiastic basketball booster who had played and coached in Belgrade and had been a member of the Yugoslav national team in the early 1950s, was particularly enchanted with the notion. What the far-sighted Stankovic saw, and what other near-sighted types (including most basketball journalists) did not, was that basketball could not truly become an international force if its marquee entity—the NBA—was not involved. Yes, it was a big deal within the Soviet Union that it had beaten the U.S., a team comprised of college players, in the 1988 semifinals in Seoul and walked away with the gold medal. But it wasn't a big deal anywhere else, not as long as everyone knew that such a defeat would not have occurred had Michael Jordan, Magic Johnson, and Larry Bird been playing for the U.S.

Indeed, the NBA at that time was at its zenith. The domestic populace could still get riled up by

Barkley, Bird, Johnson, and Laettner from the 1992 Dream Team.

North Carolina-Duke and Kentucky-Louisville, and the Final Four was one of our nation's unifying events. But around the world college hoops—any other kind of hoops—was virtually unknown because the brightest stars in the constellation were playing in the pros. Even to U.S. fans, always more resistant to the NBA than to Major League Baseball and the NFL, the personalities with the cross-marketing appeal were from the NBA.

The Stankovics in the European community also knew something that the average American basketball follower did not—the Europeans were not *that* far behind. Within the U.S., the strong international teams, such as the Soviet aggregation that had defeated the Americans in the controversial 1972 gold medal game in Munich, or the 1988 team that won in Seoul, were looked at as cyclical anomalies. Over the long haul, the U.S. would always be, as we saw it, the only game in town, *town*, in this case, being the world. But that wasn't reality.

NBA-ready players were already being turned out in Yugoslavia, Brazil, Argentina, and Spain, besides the soon-to-disintegrate Soviet Union. Stankovic's argument was this: Let the NBA stars participate. Let them dominate even. But even if it takes a decade we will be the better for it. We will have learned to play the game at the highest level and come out at the other end with an improved global product, one that could challenge soccer as a global force.

FIBA's enthusiasm for the pros' Olympic inclusion put the NBA in an extremely advantageous position: It could sit back, continually remind everyone that *this wasn't our idea*, and let

Michael Jordan, Larry Bird (opposite) and several of their NBA brethren were the first professionals to play in the Olympic Games for the U.S.

FIBA drive a horse that the league wanted driven anyway. And make no mistake about it: Though the league knew that arguments about turning an amateur endeavor over to millionaire pros were inevitable, making a truly global statement could only help *grow the game*, one of Commissioner David Stern's favorite phrases. And though there was strong resistance within the amateur community to "NBA-izing" the roster—we had, after all, won every gold medal since 1936 (the year that basketball had become an Olympic sport) except for '72 and '88—the loss in Seoul had gone down hard. Really hard. Seoul had represented an opportunity to avenge the controversial '72 game in Germany, one that still roiled in the bellies of the American Olympic community since the Soviets had gotten three chances to score the game-winning basket. When it didn't happen, the idea of some redemptive butt-kicking became a popular one.

Inevitably, FIBA voted on April 7, 1989, to lift the ban on NBA players. Officially, USA Basketball, the organization that had emerged from the alphabet-soup mix of the past to run our Olympic hoops program, cast its vote against NBA inclusion. But by then everyone knew that Stankovic had twisted enough arms to get it passed.

He and Stern had a deep and abiding mutual respect, even if their goals were not exactly the same. Stern envisioned that his league would exponentially increase its global appeal by playing in the Olympics. Stankovic envisioned that his baby—the international game—would exponentially improve its product. "From 1936 to 1972 the target for all others nations in the Olympics was second place," Stankovic said.

"Since 1972 it has not been so, and it will be the same pattern now. Right now the United States is certainly the strongest. But the world will catch up."

That latter theory was of little or no concern within our borders, for there were myriad other questions. Would the college community be left out entirely after five decades of carrying the flag? Would NBA players want to participate in what was essentially a lose-only situation? Would they give up their precious summer down time? How would they be chosen? Could already established stars be subjected to the Olympic-trial process, which in the past had eliminated players as talented as Charles Barkley? And who would be in charge? The NBA? Or USA Basketball?

Overcoming these obstacles was, obviously, a process. Russ Granik, the NBA's respected deputy commissioner and the man who sitteth at the right hand of Stern, was named a vice president of USA Basketball. In other words, it's still USA Basketball's organization, but we have our guy in there. Rod Thorn, the NBA's deputy director of operations, the third most important player in the hierarchy and a recognized "basketball guy," was tasked with finding out, often behind the scenes, who was interested in playing. It was decided fairly early that trials just wouldn't work; imagine asking, say, Isiah Thomas and John Stockton to battle it out at point guard when they had already battled it out so many times before. Barkley said flatly, "I'm not trying out." And don't even think about asking Jordan to come to camp.

It was also decided that one roster spot would be reserved for a collegian, a nod to the past. It was assumed from the outset that it would be largely a ceremonial choice, which is what it turned out to be.

Almost as important a choice as who would play was: Who could coach this band of all-stars, each one a Fortune 500 company all by himself? Among the strongest candidates was Pat Riley, who had won multiple NBA championships with the Lakers. Others were steady-as-he-goes Lenny Wilkens and the Mad Scientist of the NBA, Don Nelson. But when Detroit coach Chuck Daly was announced as the committee's choice near the end of the '91 NBA season, one in which his Bad Boys Pistons would finally fall to Jordan's Chicago Bulls, virtually everyone shook his head in assent and said, "Right guy."

Daly was the right guy for several reasons. He believed he got the gig because he was "a basketball lifer," someone who had coached at every level, a true believer who had swept the gym floors, done the dirty recruiting work, scouted, schemed, learned, and eventually earned his way to the highest level. That's true. But Daly was also considered a master handler of players, as evidenced by the fact that not only had he kept his sanity after coaching the volatile Pistons but he also had their respect.

For guiding these Olympians, after all, would not be primarily about figuring out whether to run the flex offense or a zone-press defense. It would be about those two initials that have ruined many a pro coach: PT. Playing Time. PT is a problem even on mediocre NBA teams where there might be one All-Star, one near-All-Star, six others to complete an eight-man rotation and four bench-warmers who all see themselves as the next Jordan. By contrast, Daly would be coaching a team with 11 All-Stars and one All-American, and he would have eight fewer minutes (the Olympic game is two 20-minute halves compared to the four 12-minute quarters in the NBA) to get them all in.

So Granik and Thorn began to put out their feelers. The party line was that all contacted players responded positively, and, while that's largely true, it doesn't mean that some didn't need convincing. Larry Bird, for example, was getting near retirement and suffered from an aching back. Jordan loved his offseason golf.

In February of 1991, *Sports Illustrated* ran a cover story, written by this correspondent, which began with the words: "It's a red, white, and blue dream: the five players who grace this week's cover playing together, determined to restore America's basketball dignity, in the 1992 Olympics in Barcelona." The five players on the cover were the ones I had selected as the potential starting five in Barcelona: Michael Jordan, Magic Johnson, Patrick Ewing, Charles Barkley, and Karl Malone. Over the cover photo ran the phrase "Dream Team."

And so "Dream Team" entered the vernacular, and over the years I have been given credit as coining the phrase. I didn't. Perhaps using the

Magic Johnson

Charles Barkley

word "dream" had prompted the idea, but a headline writer in the *SI* office (I've been unable to find out precisely who because that is usually a group process) put it together. Later, someone threatened to sue me because he claimed that he had copyrighted the phrase "Dream Team" and resented me making so much money from it. I never made a penny, of course, and why the hell would I have?

At any rate, the team became known as the Dream Team, and, as befitting such a regal name, its constituents were announced to much fanfare in a nationally-televised NBC show on Sept. 13, 1991. Anonymity was the lot of most U.S. Olympic athletes, even those whom Fate tapped on the shoulder (sprinters, swimmers, and female gymnasts, mostly) and went on to become three-week VIPs. Clearly, this was going to be something different.

No one could argue with the 10 selected players announced on that night. In order of fame at that time (okay, it's my order), they were: Michael Jordan, Magic Johnson, Larry Bird, Charles Barkley, Scottie Pippen, Karl Malone, Patrick Ewing, John Stockton, David Robinson, and Chris Mullin. There is simply no argument about the first three. I put Barkley fourth because he was, well, Barkley. Pippen is next because the Bulls were front and center on the NBA scene at that time. One could argue that Malone, a stalwart in Utah, would be behind Ewing, a stalwart in New York, but I see it this way. Stockton is next, mainly because neither Robinson (Spurs) nor Mullins (Warriors) played for marquee teams. (Obviously, that would change with Robinson.)

The main controversy, predictably, was over who *wasn't* on the team—Isiah Thomas and Joe Dumars, both of whom had been stars for Daly on the Pistons' two championship teams. Dumars was a borderline choice from the outset (though with a multiplicity of skills and a team-first personality he would've been an exceptional fit), but Thomas was a legit elite player, quite possibly the most talented little man in the history of the game. But he was also unpopular with some players, most notably Jordan. The party line is that neither Daly nor Jordan had a voice in picking personnel. I buy that in the case of Daly, although early in the process he did select his wish list of players, which according to my best sources had put Thomas right behind Magic at point guard. But I don't buy that Jordan, a reluctant joiner at the outset, did not strongly hint that he might not be a Dream Teamer if Thomas were to be a teammate.

The final two players were added in May, about two months before the team was to congregate for its first training camp. Portland's Clyde Drexler, an immense talent, was a popular addition. (Though not in Detroit, where fans, and Thomas, wondered why he was not the guy, particularly since Thomas's Pistons had torched Drexler's Blazers with three on-the-road wins in the '89 Finals.) The college pick was not so popular — Duke's Christian Laettner. Like Thomas, Laettner was a lightning rod for criticism, a surly oncourt personality who seemed to enjoy playing the villain. Further, many observers believed that his pro upside was not high and certainly not as high as the other Dream Team possibility, LSU's Shaquille O'Neal. But Laettner was absolutely the right choice. A four-year warrior, he remains one of the best college players of all-time, and it was only fair that he got the spot.

In late June at the University of San Diego, hundreds of journalists who would've never dreamed of covering an Olympic practice session waited for their first glimpse of the Dream Team together. On one level, the off-the-charts interest was strange because seeing these players together was not a novelty. Jordan-Pippen and Malone-Stockton were teammates during the season. Bird and Magic had made commercials together. So had Jordan and Bird. Jordan and Barkley palled around in the offseason. And most of them had been teammates at one time or another in All-Star games.

But there was something about them all being together *on one team*, all those bright lights burning together for one cause. You took their individual fame quotients, added them together and multiplied by—what?—a hundred? A thousand? That was the Dream Team in the summer months before the Barcelona Games. The fascination factor (FF) was immense, almost like, say, the Stones, the Who and the E Street Band had gotten together for a worldwide tour, the collision of constellations producing questions. Who would play lead guitar—Keith Richard, Pete Townsend or Bruce? So who would play the metaphorical lead guitar on the Dream Team? Who would be the leader? Who would compromise his game? Would old rivalries surface? Which teammates wouldn't get along?

Answers weren't always easy to come by, for the Dreamers, befitting Olympic rules and also strict security measures that had to be enacted because of the collective celebrity of the personalities involved, practiced under a veil of secrecy that only added to the FF. Chuck Daly put it to the team this way in their first meeting: "Our next six weeks," he said, "is a Tom Clancy novel waiting to happen."

Scrimmages were intense, partly because the players involved were intense, partly because the invited competition wanted to prove that it, too, could've joined this august bunch and one day might be NBA Olympians. Those young players included Penny Hardaway, Grant Hill, Chris Webber, Bobby Hurley, and Allan Houston. Word filtered out immediately when the Dream Teamers lost a scrimmage, 62-54 … and up went the FF.

Because the U.S. had failed to win the gold in Seoul, it had to enter a qualifying tournament in Portland, something now akin to telling Tiger Woods that he has to go through Monday morning qualifying. But, really, it was a blessing. It gave the Dream Team members a chance to find their roles before the real international stage and gave the NBA a pre-Olympic chance to market before the mega-marketing began.

The scene at the Coliseum in Portland on the Sunday afternoon of June 28 was electric. Hardened journalists who normally stayed in the pressroom until the first tip-off (and sometimes beyond) were in their seats early. The seats were filled—no pregame hotdogs and hold that trip to the bathroom. But what really stamped the occasion as different was the behavior of the opponent, Cuba, as it turned out, a nation with which we don't even have diplomatic relations. As the Cubans went through their pregame layup line,

they sometimes simply stopped and cast anxious glances toward the other end of the floor.

Finally, out they came, Magic, who had been named co-captain with Bird, leading the way. The crowd stood and roared. Flashbulbs burst. The Cuban warmup disintegrated as the players simply gaped. They requested a photo op *before* tipoff. "That's a new one," Chris Mullin would say later. The overall ambience was carnival-like, but the Americans wore a look of collective seriousness. And then Daly sent out the first Dream Team starters, a symbolic milestone: Jordan, Magic, Bird, Barkley, and Robinson. At this point in his career, Bird was probably not one of the five best players, but he deserved to be there, next to his good buddy and old rival, Magic, and next to the man to whom he and Magic had handed the baton, Jordan. Barkley was an obvious choice, but it's possible that Ewing would've started over Robinson had the Knicks center not dislocated his thumb in La Jolla.

Bird took a pass from Magic and scored the first Dream Team basket. "I knew I had to shoot," he joked later, "because I was afraid I wouldn't get the ball again." So much for the basketball talk. The odd thing about the Dream Team is that once their games began there was precious little valuable information to report. They were over early. All of them. There is no strategy to dissect and too many magic moments to chronicle. The U.S. won its first qualifying game against Cuba 136-57, its last one 127-80 over Venezuela and the ones in between over Panama, Argentina, and Puerto Rico by an average of 46.3 points.

What must be understood is the sense of mission with which the Dream Team approached its task. It's not that losing wasn't an option. Of course it wasn't. It was that being *challenged* for even a meaningful stretch of the game wasn't an option. You send that message out to a bunch of competitive, ultra-talented, and mature players and what you get is a team that suffocates the opposition, never giving it a chance.

The texture of the games is what resonated. Opponents asking for autographs. Visiting journalists leaning their heads into postgame photos. Marcelo Milanesio, a guard for Argentina, asking Magic for his jersey *before* the game, and continuing to pester him throughout. *I must have your jersey, Ma-jeek. I must have your jersey.* He never got it, but after the game Milanesio exclaimed: "I am so overwhelmed by joy." That after being on the wrong end of a 128-87 butt-kicking.

The carnival moved, appropriately enough, to Monte Carlo, where the Dream Team held its five-day pre-Olympic Camp G2—golf and gambling. Jordan and Daly hit the links almost every day together, and Barkley, who at that time was not victimized by his tortured swing, Drexler and Robinson got out there, too. Many of the players brought their families and plenty of craps and roulette money. Let's be honest here: Traveling to Monte Carlo to practice basketball is akin to traveling to the Seychelles to study for finals.

Chuck Daly

Yet it was in Monte Carlo that the Dream Teamers put the final layer of polish on their Olympic shoes during a pickup game that has become legendary. Again, it went unwitnessed by the media but was duly reported as the all-time smack-talking session, Jordan on one side, Magic on the other. Jordan's team, which included Malone, Robinson, Pippen and Laettner, fell behind 14-2 to Magic's team, which included Bird, Barkley, Ewing, and Mullin. (Drexler and Stockton were out with injuries.) But back came the Jordanaires, Michael leading the way, jabbering all the time, his team finally emerging with a 40-36 victory that, to Jordan, felt almost as sweet as the NBA championship he and Pippen had won a month earlier against the Trail Blazers. After the win, Jordan ran around the corner, singing (though his voice does not match his basketball talent) "Sometimes I dream," a song from one of his most famous Gatorade commercials. To be the best of the best, well, that was something.

And that Jordan proved to be. To the observers who followed the team from San Diego to Portland to Monte Carlo to Barcelona— including myself—it was on the Dream Team that Jordan truly proved his preeminence. He was the best shooter, the best passer, the best defender, the best everything. Though Chuck

Daly was loathe to admit it publicly, the coach could wax breathlessly about Jordan's supremacy as a player, something that could be demonstrated only among other great players.

But there was one thing Jordan could not do: Once in Barcelona, he could not bring the joy the way one teammate could.

Barcelona had never seen anything like it. All you need to know about the Dream Team's arrival in Barcelona is this: More than 1,000 media members showed up at their introductory press conference, many of whom (the international press anyway) stood and applauded when the Dreamers sauntered in. "These are the stars from the stars," remarked Arturas Karnisovas, a forward from Lithuania, which was one of two teams (along with Croatia) considered talented enough to give the U.S. a game.

It's easy to compress the Olympic basketball "suspense" into one sentence, too: The U.S. beat eight teams by an average of 43.8 points (eight fewer than the margin by which it had prevailed in Portland) and won the final two decisive games over worthy opponents (Lithuania and Croatia) by 127-76 and 117-85. Enough said. All right a little more: The best non-American player was Lithuania's Sarunas Marciulionis, by then an established NBA player with the Golden State Warriors. Daly assigned Jordan the task of shutting him down to begin the second half of the semifinal game. During a six-minute stretch, Marciulionis could barely get the ball, never mind get off a shot. Game over.

All right a little more. At this time, the Bulls were pursuing Toni Kukoc, the 6'11" versatile southpaw who starred for Croatia, the Dream Team's

opponent in the gold medal final. That pursuit was delaying Pippen's contract renegotiation. Daly knew exactly who to put on Kukoc; with Pippen dogging him, Kukoc made only two of 11 shots. Game over.

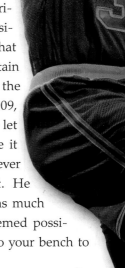

Patrick Ewing

Daly had joked before the Olympics that he had three goals—never to call a timeout (he didn't), never to stand and pace during games (he didn't) and never to miss a tee time (he didn't). He joked before the Croatia game that he was going to limit Jordan to nine holes, so wary was he of his opponent.

But Daly took the games seriously, too. He knew the opposition personnel, he knew what buttons to push to get a certain player motivated. In short, the coach, who died in May of 2009, struck just the right note. He let it be known what a pleasure it was to coach the team and never stepped forward for credit. He treated his opponents with as much respect as circumstances deemed possible. (Imagine going deep into your bench to keep the score down and coming up with, say, David Robinson.)

The general impression left by the Dream Team, however, wasn't all positive. The world was still uncertain about the repercussions of Magic Johnson's having the AIDS virus, a revelation that had become public two months after he was announced as a Dream Team member. Ignorance of the disease, after all, was not limited to the United States.

Because players and their families, coaches, and league execs were ensconced in a luxury hotel with around-the-clock security, the distinction between the Dreamers and the other Olympians began to be duly noted and duly recorded. Jim Courier, at that time among the world's top-ranked tennis players, was so conscious of being accorded amenities not available to other Olympians that he moved out of his hotel and into the Olympic Village. When asked about that option, the Dream Teamers pretty much said, "Are you kidding?"

Some athletes and Olympic officials began to resent the fact that the basketball competition—which wasn't really competition anyway—began to overshadow the other more traditional sports such as track and field and swimming. Every U.S. game was an event, the equivalent of a mini-Super Bowl, everything screeching to a stop as the Dream Teamers left their luxury digs, rode on their luxury bus, summarily dispatched the opposition and climbed back on the bus under cover of darkness. The Dream Teamers couldn't do much about that, of course. But near the end of the Games, the story line became about whether or not the athletes under contract to

Nike, Jordan most prominently, would deign to wear the "platform ceremony" uniform designed by adidas, which had made a deal with the USOC. Thus, was the semi-commercial nature of the whole enterprise made clear, if it wasn't before.

But, then, there was Charles Barkley. He alone of the Dream Teamers became a Barcelona personality, spending his off nights wandering Las Ramblas, Barcelona's main drag, gathering various hangers-on, stopping at watering holes, signing autographs, a nocturnal Pied Piper. It was almost forgotten that Barkley, the one loose cannon among all that American firepower, had thrown an elbow at a skinny forward from Angola in the opening game.

In fact, the loose elbow had its positive side. For it demonstrated that the Americans were there to take care of business. Had the Dream Team lah-de-dahed through the tournament, turning the gas on and off, playing capriciously only when the spirit moved them, it would've been an insult to the rest of the competition.

And so—finally, inevitably—the Americans received their gold medals (Jordan casually draped a towel around his adidas logo) and, eventually, a small share of the world's GNP in endorsement deals. The NBA got a shot in the arm from the strong showing. The American basketball community got back its pride.

But what transpired, in the final analysis, went well beyond all that. The U.S. domination presented to the world a basketball paradigm, a blueprint, if you will, for excellence. And all those young Dirk Nowitzskis in Germany and Manu Ginobilis in Argentina were watching, learning

and starting to think, "I can be those guys some day." Though few had the foresight to realize it at the time—figuring the Dream Team rout to be only the first of what would become a long interrupted string of U.S. routs—Boris Stankovic had seen the future. The U.S. conquered the world … but the world had won.

Kentucky: College Basketball's First National Attraction

By Blair Kerkhoff

Sports provided emotional escape during the economic Depression of the 1930s and the games were important enough to continue when war tore the world apart in the 1940s.

It was a time when America's sports interests expanded and college basketball started to find its legs, emerging from pockets of local interest to begin gaining a national audience.

One program showed the way:

Kentucky.

Before the UCLA dynasty or North Carolina's sustained magnificence, Kentucky became the first face of college basketball, the first to be recognized widely for its greatness, and it filled a state with immense pride along the way.

A citizen's ownership in this team is where the explanation of the phenomenon that is Kentucky basketball begins. Winning basketball brought together a state of dramatic contrasts. The coal miner from the east regions of Kentucky cheered for the same team as the aristocrat from horse country. At Alumni Gym, and later at Memorial Coliseum, the gas station guy from Pikeville could sit next to the bank president from Louisville, or even the starlet from Los Angeles.

Ashley Judd, a diehard Wildcats fan, is "just folk" at Kentucky games and she doesn't simply act the part. Once she was offered a jacket with a North Carolina logo on a chilly movie set. "I would just as soon freeze to death," Judd said.

Stories of Kentucky faith and passion abound. Famed radio voice of the Wildcats Cawood Ledford told the story of a pilot flying over eastern Kentucky around 2 a.m., and noticing how nearly every house in the small towns had lights on. He called the tower in Lexington and learned Kentucky was playing a tournament in Alaska at the time, several time zones away.

A teenage driver in Harlan County once swerved to avoid hitting a dog and struck a utility pole, knocking out power in a couple of towns as a Kentucky basketball game was about to be aired. The investigating officer refused to identify the boy for fear of fan retribution.

Kentucky fans like to cite a *Louisville Courier-Journal* poll in which half of the folks who identified themselves as college basketball fans cheered for Kentucky, and the other half for the hometown Louisville Cardinals.

They don't like to remember a *Lexington Herald-Leader* series of stories in 1985 on scandal in the basketball program that won a Pulitzer Prize. Hundreds canceled their newspaper subscription. A bomb threat was called into the newspaper's office, and street corner vending machines were shot up.

Kentucky is where a fan once camped for 41 days to be at the front of the line … for the opening night practice!

This devotion can be traced to one man and one moment in time. Adolph Rupp, "the Baron of the Bluegrass," came along in 1930 and began to give Kentucky a national identity other than poverty, coal mines and the Hatfields and McCoys.

Unlike other states in the South, Kentucky couldn't count on football to lift its spirits. The Wildcats on the gridiron had been dismal, and there had been talk of leaving its conference affiliation for lack of competitiveness.

Kentucky had its Derby, fine bourbon and not much else going for it when Rupp, in his famous brown suits, arrived in Lexington with a background that portended success.

He grew up in Halstead, Kansas, and was good enough to make the varsity squad at the University of Kansas, although not good enough to crack the lineup for teams in 1922 and 1923 that were retroactively named national champions. Rupp was part of the "Meat Packers," the reserves who played when the game was no longer in doubt.

But he learned plenty from the experience. Phog Allen, one of the game's first great figures, was his coach, and James Naismith, basketball's inventor, was Rupp's physical education instructor and a friend to all the players.

Adolph Rupp transformed the Kentucky Wildcats into a national attraction.

Kansas had one of the nation's top programs in the 1920s, but college basketball in the national perspective was just background noise. The game was popular on campus, but without a postseason tournament, teams played for the conference title and called it a year.

The excitement and news was produced in the regular season, and for much of the 1930s, New York City was the game's attention base and its most influential figure was a sportswriter and promoter who saw college basketball's great marketing potential.

Ned Irish moved games from small New York gyms into Madison Square Garden for doubleheaders and created a phenomenon. Legend has it that in 1933, Irish arrived late to a Manhattan College game only to find the doors locked. He crawled through a window and ripped his pants, but he realized the game's money-making potential in larger venues.

Irish had the idea of bringing in outside competition to face New York teams, and he wanted Kentucky, which had started to pile up Southern Conference championships almost immediately under Rupp.

And the Baron didn't need much persuading. He had spent four summers at Columbia University and loved the city. New York sportswriters couldn't get enough of Rupp. They wined and dined him—Rupp never picked up a check—and in return received colorful quotes.

Kentucky's game against New York University got terrific media buzz because the Wildcats had won their first four games of the 1934-35 season by scores of 81-12, 38-9, 52-12 and 42-16. But in the Garden, the Wildcats fell to NYU, 23-22.

Still, Irish and the New Yorkers were impressed and Rupp's early teams returned to the Big Apple when they could for doubleheaders or games against Long Island University.

Rupp loved to show off his team and was one of the first coaches to understand the concept of good press. The Wildcats traveled to Chicago, Detroit, Omaha and Philadelphia in the 1930s, with Rupp meeting reporters at every stop.

Kentucky usually won. Beating the slow-paced teams in the South was one thing, but winning in the big cities had a dramatic impact on the program and the home folks. The fellows with "Kentucky" on their uniforms came back winners to a state that had a difficult time thinking of itself as a winner.

At the same time another force helped move college basketball forward. This was radio's golden age.

With a quarter of the nation unemployed, radio helped people leave behind their troubles for a few hours while sitting around their wooden box in the living room. How important was radio during the Depression? Social workers found that people sold their refrigerators, beds, and other possessions to pay bills but they would not sell their radios.

With the nation looking for good news, the conditions were ideal for a program to step into the national sporting consciousness in a way no other college basketball team had. Baseball had its Yankees and Cardinals. College football had Notre Dame and Minnesota.

As the Depression gave way to World War II, Kentucky was the college basketball brand beamed into homes across America.

Rupp's 1932 team finished tied for first in what was then the Southern Conference. His next five teams would win the conference outright. People were curious about this team that didn't seem to have much trouble dispensing with the competition every year.

By the end of the 1930s, only Long Island had a greater winning percentage for the decade than Kentucky, and the Wildcats would top college basketball in winning ratio in the 1940s and 1950s, and in total victories over those 20 years as well.

Kentucky had won before Rupp. The man he replaced, John Mauer, had just won a school-record 16 games and piled up a record of 40-14 in his three seasons.

Rupp brought with him a massive ego and dedication to excellence.

But he almost didn't get there.

Rupp considered giving up basketball after his fourth season at Freeport High in Illinois. He thought about becoming a school administrator because they made more money, and the Kentucky coach had just stepped down because he hadn't gotten a pay raise.

But off he went to Lexington and became an immediate success. With the boys operating a fast break offense, the Wildcats beat Georgetown, Kentucky, 67-19 in his first game.

Players who didn't work hard in practice were shown the door, and players on Rupp's early teams say practice was more difficult than any game.

"The first thing you have to do," Rupp once said, "is curtail the individual desire of the boy in the interest of team play. Then you have to correct two deficiencies every boy has—in playing defense and recognizing the value of ball possession."

Practices went from 3:30 to 5 p.m., and began with 30 minutes of spot shooting and ended with 15 minutes of free-throw shooting. There were no sounds other than squeaking sneakers, balls bouncing and Rupp's instructions.

Once, Governor Happy Chandler attended practice and Rupp heard him laugh. According to author Russell Rice in his book *Adolph Rupp, Kentucky's Basketball Baron,* Rupp snapped. "I don't care if you are the governor. Either be quiet or get out."

At every practice, Rupp and his assistant coaches dressed in pressed khakis. Players wore indistinguishable white undershirts, shoes, socks, and shorts.

In the early years, Rupp rarely warmed up to his players. Alex Groza told *Sports Illustrated* writer Frank Deford in 1966 that on his national champi-

onship teams of the late 1940s "there was no joking, no laughing, no whistling, no singing, no nothing. Just basketball. When we traveled, he often communicated with us through the team manager."

Players rarely received praise. Since they played for Rupp they were supposed to be good. And sarcasm and criticism were part of Rupp's lexicon.

"My, Gawd, you just made the worst mistake since this building has been built. Burn the damn thing down if you're going to play defense like that," he'd say with a distinctive nasal twang. Or, "Please send me someone who is worth a damn."

One of his favorite put-downs would embarrass a player in practice: "Son, I'm going to write a book about how not to play basketball, and I'm going to devote the first 200 pages to you."

If he talked to his players that way, imagine what he said about opponents and officials. During a 1934 blowout victory at Tulane, Rupp barked at one of his players for allowing an opponent to score, which reduced an 18-point lead to 16. Boos rained down on Rupp.

After that one-point loss to NYU at Madison Square Garden in 1935, Rupp claimed that officials had to ensure New York University won a home game to maintain the city's interest in the sport.

There was never any doubt about who was in charge, basketball or otherwise, at Kentucky. In 1968, Rupp was informed that he'd have to change a practice time because it conflicted with a speech vice-presidential candidate Edmund Muskie was to deliver in Memorial Coliseum.

Rupp seethed: "If Muskie stops a Kentucky practice he'll lose votes here."

Muskie changed the date of his speech.

All of this was tolerated because Rupp's teams produced. The Wildcats won their first national tournament by taking the 1946 NIT, when that event rivaled the NCAA Tournament in importance.

But 1948 became a watershed year. The Fabulous Five of Alex Groza, Ralph Beard, Wallace "Wah Wah" Jones, Cliff Barker and Kenny Rollins, won the first of two straight NCAA titles with a blazing fast-break style.

After the 1948 championship, the Kentucky starters made up half of the Olympic team that captured the gold medal in London. Rupp was an assistant coach and receiving his medal at Wembley Stadium was one of the proudest moments of his life.

A shameful one quickly followed. In 1952, a grand jury in New York charged 33 college players with taking money from gamblers to shave points, and among those who confessed were three stars from Rupp's first two title teams: Beard, Groza, and Dale Barnstable.

It was Rupp who once said gamblers "couldn't touch my boys with a ten-foot pole." He was so humiliated by the episode he didn't speak to the players for nearly 20 years.

The Wildcats became college sports' first "death penalty" program when Kentucky was forced to sit out the entire 1952-53 season because of rules violations, including payments to players by boosters, which were uncovered during the points-shaving investigation.

The scandal isn't the only tarnish on Rupp's legacy. The 1966 championship game pitted his all-white Wildcats against the all-black starting five of Texas Western. The game, won by the Miners, and its aftermath cast Rupp as a racist who wouldn't recruit African-American players although there is evidence in his career to support that he wasn't racist, including having a black player on his Illinois high school team.

That's not how most Kentuckians remember Rupp. He is the coach who in 42 years won 876 games, a record eventually broken by Dean

> My Gawd, you just made the worst **mistake** since this building has been built. Burn the damn thing down if you're going to play defense like that.
>
> — Adolph Rupp

Dean Smith eventually surpassed Adolph Rupp in career wins.

his guys they would to have to live with the shame of that defeat for the rest of their lives.

Everyone who played for Rupp told a story about a man who defined old school coaching. They feared him, loathed him and when they were finished, they revered him.

Rupp changed how a state felt about itself. College sports can do that. Football helped Oklahoma shed its reputation as a Dust Bowl wasteland and Bear Bryant's success at Alabama made people look at that state in ways other than civil rights conflict.

And Rupp in the 1930s and 1940s helped start college basketball's mass appeal and prompted the nation to look at Kentucky as a state that could be good at something.

It was his greatest accomplishment.

Smith and Bob Knight, and four national championships.

He's the coach whose teams were immortalized in nicknames: "The Fabulous Five," "The Fiddlin Five" (Rupp once said his team might be pretty good barnyard fiddlers but had a Carnegie Hall schedule and would need to be violinists to win), and "Rupp's Runts," the undersized 1966 championship runners-up.

He was the coach whose teams won a remarkable NCAA-record 129 consecutive home games, and after the Wildcats lost to Georgia Tech in 1955 Rupp, in typical Rupp fashion, told

Nothing means anything if you don't win everything

By David DuPree

Dynasties are hard to build, difficult to maintain, and it's nearly impossible for them to withstand the scrutiny of time.

Everything has to fall perfectly into place, with the right players, coming together at the right time, with the right coach, and the right set of intangibles.

Enter the Chicago Bulls, a rather pedestrian franchise that, after entering the NBA in 1966, had only six winning seasons in its first 18 years in the league with no NBA titles and nary even a visit to the Finals.

Then, with the third pick of the 1984 draft, after having won only 27 games the previous season, a clean cut young man from North Carolina named Michael Jeffrey Jordan fell into the Bulls' laps.

The Houston Rockets, picking first in the draft, selected center Hakeem Olajuwon. The Portland Trail Blazers, picking second, were torn between Jordan and Sam Bowie. But since they already had and were very pleased with Clyde Drexler, who played the same position as Jordan, they went for size and took Bowie, a 7'1" center from Kentucky.

That left Jordan for the Bulls.

The team and the NBA as a whole were changed forevermore.

Jordan was an instant hit, quickly proving to be an exciting individual star, and season-by-season, piece-by-piece, a team of greatness was built around him. Then, going into Jordan's fourth season in the league, the Bulls hit it big in the 1987 draft, selecting Horace Grant with the 10th pick, and trading Olden Polynice, who they had drafted with the eighth pick, to the Seattle SuperSonics for a relative unknown from little Central Arkansas by the name of Scottie Pippen.

Three seasons later Phil Jackson was named head coach.

MJ changed his uniform number from 23 to 45 after returning from a brief retirement.

The many faces of Jordan during his best years with the Chicago Bulls.

A dynasty was hatched, and all of a sudden, the 90s belonged to the Chicago Bulls, heirs to the NBA's legacy chain previously dominated by the Los Angles Lakers, Boston Celtics, and Detroit Pistons, who from 1980 through 1990 had combined for 10 of 11 league championships, the Lakers winning five titles, the Celtics three, and the Pistons two.

The Bulls would do even better.

They won their first title in 1991 and completed the NBA's first three-peat in a quarter century as they won again in 1992 and 1993. Jordan left the game to try his hand at baseball, missing the entire 1993-94 season and most of the 1994-95 campaign. When he returned to the NBA full time, he led the Bulls to their second three-peat of the decade with league titles in 1996, 1997, and 1998.

Hall of Famer Magic Johnson summed up what the Bulls were like in the 90s when he said, "The thing is that of course you have to stop Michael, but that doesn't even guarantee a win. All you can do against them is try to play a perfect game and hope they have a bad one."

Jordan, considered by many to be the greatest player ever, not only defined the Bulls, but defined the NBA in that era. He was the face of the league and it was understandable why everyone wanted to be like Mike. In addition to the six championships, he won 10 scoring titles – a record seven in a row in one stretch – and was the league's MVP five times. He displayed a rare combination of athletic ability, desire, steel nerves, and a relentless attitude to be the best. He coupled all of that with a tireless work ethic, an insatiable need to win, and the cut-throat attitude that he felt left him to control the fate of both himself and his team.

It was Steve Kerr, a teammate of Jordan's throughout the second three-peat, who put what it was like to play with Jordan in perspective. "Michael is clearly head and shoulders above everybody else, even the other All-Stars," Kerr said following his first season with Jordan. "Most nights he simply will not let us lose."

Jordan never was one to sing his own praises, however.

"I have this special ability," is about as far as he would go in talking about his own greatness. "Away from the game, I just wanted to fit in," he said, "but on the court, I was all business."

His mark on the sport goes far beyond the scoring titles, the championships, and the records. He has never been a follower, either. There was always a way, then another way and then the Jordan way to do things. He's the one who set the pace, made the style, and established the trend. The bald head, baggy shorts and shorter socks were all started by Jordan.

"If I had an influence on styles with those things, then so be it," Jordan said. "But it never was my goal to do those things. I was just being me."

Jordan never was one for comparisons and normally has left it to others to define the place his Bulls of the 90s should take in NBA lore.

"The historians will decide our place among the greatest teams," Jordan said during the final season of their remarkable run to six titles in eight seasons, "but we certainly accomplished everything we set out to do."

Had it not been for Jordan's fling at baseball, the Bulls very well could have won eight titles in a row and silenced all skepticism about them being the greatest team ever. "There are a lot of opinions about who the greatest team is," Jordan said after the Bulls won their third straight championship in 1993. "You look at the Boston Celtics, who won 16 championships (eight in a row), and they certainly have to be considered a great team. But with so much talent and parity in the league now, we have to be considered one of the greatest teams ever. Individually, we may not have the greatest players, but I'll take this team against any team from any era. I don't care what anybody says."

Little did Jordan know that when he spoke those words that three seasons later, after his baseball career was over, another Bulls team led by Jackson, Pippen, and himself would stir the team to make *dynasty* the only word that properly captured Chicago's accomplishments.

After the first three-peat team was broken up by Jordan's retirement, the pack caught up with the Bulls. But when Jordan came back for a full season in 1996, with a whole new cast of characters from their first three-peat years, except for Pippen, the Bulls would re-write the record books. They set a standard for winning and dominance that would bring opponents and critics to their knees.

The 1996-97 Bulls became the first NBA team to win 70 games and finished 72-10. They won by an average of more than 12 points a game and led the league in scoring with 105.2 a game. They breezed through the playoffs, winning 15 of 18 games.

The Larry O'Brien NBA Championship Trophy wasn't the only hardware the Bulls took home that season. Jordan won the regular season MVP, All-Star MVP, and NBA Finals MVP in addition to winning the league scoring title. Jordan and Pippen made the All-NBA First Team and Dennis Rodman, the league's leading rebounder, joined them on the All-Defensive First Team. Toni Kukoc won the Sixth Man Award, Jackson was the Coach of the Year, and general manager Jerry Krause was the Executive of the Year.

Another sign of their dominance is that they beat five different teams in their pair of three-peats. After defeating the Los Angeles Lakers, Portland Trail Blazers, Phoenix Suns, and Seattle SuperSonics, the Bulls closed out the run with wins against the Utah Jazz in 1997 and 1998.

By comparison, when the Celtics won their eighth championship in a row in 1966, there were only nine teams in the league and five of them had losing records. The playoffs were only three rounds and Boston faced the Lakers five times in the Finals in that eight-year period. When the Bulls completed their second three-peat, in 1998, the league had grown to 29 teams and the playoffs had expanded to four rounds. That made their road to the top a much more treacherous path.

Never, not even in the heyday of Magic Johnson and Larry Bird, was a team as popular as the Bulls were to become. Not only did their 1998 championship series against the Jazz have the highest television ratings ever for the NBA Finals, but they also had the next four highest-rated Finals, as well. Their lowest-rated NBA Finals was 1992 against Portland and that was still the ninth highest-rated Finals series.

The coach-player relationship in any sport in any era is often tenuous, but every so often a coach and player just seem made for each other. It was that way between Red Auerbach and Bill Russell with the Celtics and it was that way between Pat Riley and Magic Johnson with the Lakers.

And it was certainly there between Phil Jackson and Michael Jordan. Few coaches and players have ever been as perfectly suited for each other as they were, and the relationship they shared was at the heart of the success of the Bulls. "There are very few opportunities in life where you find people that suit you just right," Jordan said during the second three-peat run. "Phil thinks the way I think and has an understanding of the things I do. He reminds me of Dean Smith (Jordan's coach at North Carolina). Every time I step on the court, his attitude parallels mine. He knows how to relieve some of the tension surrounding me, yet at the same time, knows the buttons to push when he feels like I'm taking a break here and there."

Dennis Rodman and the Bulls logo – two icons of the NBA during the 1990s.

Jordan could always score and was never short on confidence, but he never really became great until he learned how to make his teammates better by trusting them and getting them to believe in themselves. He learned a great deal about that aspect of the game from Jackson.

"He enhances his players' dedication to the game and their ability to be better teammates

Dennis Rodman & Scottie Pippen

and he's able to do that without taking away from your individuality," Jordan said.

Jackson has college degrees in both philosophy and religion and throw-in his self-taught psychology and you have one of the smartest and most successful coaches in NBA history. A rather nondescript player, Jackson, an angular 6'9" forward, was a reserve on the New York Knicks' 1973 NBA championship team. When it came to managing the Bulls dynasty, however, he showed that he could be both a raging Bull and a calm counselor.

"I never try to understand Phil Jackson because it could drive you crazy," said forward Horace Grant, who was a mainstay of the Bulls first three-peat run. "He tries to use a lot of psychology on us. Sometimes it works, sometimes it doesn't, but he always lets us be ourselves. He definitely understands that it's a players' game. He's straight up with you. He's not going to give you any B.S., and that's what the guys appreciate."

The next most important factor in the Bulls' dynasty was the Jordan-Pippen alliance.

Critics of Scottie Pippen often like to point out that he never won a championship without Jordan. Jordan is quick to point out that he never won one without Pippen, either.

Pippen never was the scorer Jordan was, but he was a great second option, a master facilitator, a lock-down defender and one of the most versatile players the NBA has ever seen. He and Jordan made a formidable tandem, feeding off each other at both ends of the floor, yet remark-ably staying out of each other's way, making it virtually impossible to defend them both.

"He pushed me to be the best player I could be," Pippen said when Jordan retired again after the 1998 title. "He expected things from me he didn't expect from others, and he rode me harder early in my career because he saw something special in me. He taught me about being competitive and about taking practice seriously. He also taught me to use the game to put myself at peace."

The two three-peat teams were markedly different in personnel, but mirror images in terms of style and objective.

Except for Jordan, Pippen, Jackson, and assistant coaches Tex Winter and Jim Cleamons, the team that culminated the first three-peat in 1993 was completely different from the one that began the second three-peat in the 1995-96 season. Horace Grant, B.J. Armstrong, John Paxson, Bill Cartwright, Stacey King, Darrell Walker, Trent Tucker, Will Perdue, Darrell Walker, Scott Williams, and Rodney McCray were the support-ing cast on the 1993 championship team. They were all gone when the second three-peat started, having been replaced by Croatian Kukoc, a versatile 6'10" matchup nightmare for opponents, whom the Bulls had drafted in 1990 and who had played in Europe until the 1993-94 season; power forward Rodman, who came via a trade with San Antonio for Will Perdue; center Luc Longley, whom they traded King to Minnesota to get; and a long list of free agents led by Kerr, Ron Harper, Bill Wennington, Jud Buechler, and Randy Brown. Everyone had a specific role and each played his to the max.

It was the same successful formula that led to the first three titles, only the names had been changed.

The biggest gamble was with the enigmatic Rodman, historically speaking, not a Bulls-type player. He was off in his own world much of the time, but when the bell rang, he answered it and his will to win and toughness fit right in with the Bulls' way of doing things. Not much of a scorer, Rodman was a whole lot of everything else. In his three seasons with the Bulls, he won three rebounding titles, gave the Bulls the defensive presence and toughness they needed inside, and helped them to three more titles.

Great teams have a system that they believe in and follow. With the Bulls, that was the triangle, or triple-post, offense. It was the brainchild of legendary coach Tex Winter, who perfected it over a span of 50 years. It is the most complicated, yet effective half court offense the NBA has ever seen. The Bulls were the first NBA team to make it their primary offense; Jackson bought into it early and Winter was the one who taught it.

"It's the way we teach it, not what we are teaching," Winter said of the triangle. "You can't copy it because you can't teach something you don't completely understand."

It's called the triangle because the players align in triangles on the floor and any of the five players can be in any of the spots. It starts with a pass to the post followed by a variety of cuts off it, dictated by how the defense plays. The most difficult thing in trying to defend it is that there is a counter for everything. It is predicated on what Winter calls the seven principles of sound

Scottie Pippen

Phil Jackson guided the Chicago Bulls to a regular-season record 72 wins in 1995-96 and was the NBA's Coach of the Year.

offensive basketball: penetration, spacing, ball movement, rebounding position with defensive balance, five-man concept (with options to pass to every player), the offense counters the defense, and the utilization of the individual talents of the players.

"Because of the triangle, we don't call a lot of plays," Winter added during the Bulls' 72-win season

"We key off the ball, but we have special things we can incorporate into the offense. It gives us stability and consistency."

It also utilized Jordan's skills perfectly because it kept everyone else involved when he had the ball.

"We space, but we don't isolate," Winter said.

Just as distinguishing a characteristic of the Bulls as their dominance was their mind set. They didn't set out to re-write the record books. They set out each season with one goal – to win the championship.

"In the end that's all that matters," Jordan said after his final game as a Bull, a 45-point effort in the 87-86 championship series clinching Game 6 win of the 1998 NBA Finals against the Utah Jazz. "Winning is why we play the game. Everything else that comes with it does just that – comes with it. Nothing means anything if you don't win everything."

RIVALRIES

RIVALRIES

Loving, loathing, cheering and groaning .... when rivals meet, blood boils.

Rivalries:
The Intersection
of Loving and Loathing

By Bob Ryan

It is Sunday afternoon, May 23, 1982, and the defending champion Boston Celtics are going down. There are about 30 seconds remaining in what would turn out to be a 120-106 Philadelphia 76er Game 7 triumph in the Boston Garden when a voice rings out in the upper reaches of the building.

"Beat L.A.!"

Soon, thousands take up the chant. "Beat L.A.! Beat L.A.!" No one had ever heard anything like it.

Here were the disappointed Boston fans, watching their team lose to an ancient foe, imploring said foe to inflict pain on a team they despise even more, and never mind the fact that their heroes had not even faced the other team in the playoffs for 13 years.

Magic Johnson and Larry Bird were fierce rivals on the court, but genuine friends off it.

Now *that's* a rivalry.

In the National Basketball Association there are all types of rivalries. There are natural rivals, born out of geography (e.g. Boston-New York, Dallas-San Antonio, Los Angeles-San Francisco/Oakland, Seattle-Portland). There are fierce short-term rivalries based on unique personalities and/or the intensity of clustered playoff confrontations (e.g. New York-Baltimore, New York-Miami, Boston-Buffalo, Detroit-Boston, Detroit-Chicago). There are long-term rivalries created by repeated confrontations at the highest level (e.g. Boston-Philadelphia, Boston-Los Angeles). And there are, of course, fierce individual rivalries (e.g. Chamberlain-Russell, Bird-Magic, DeBusschere-Johnson, Abdul-Jabbar-Chamberlain, Abdul-Jabbar-Thurmond, Abdul-Jabbar-Cowens, Reed-Unseld).

But let no one doubt that the two greatest have been Boston-Los Angeles on a team basis and Wilt Chamberlain-Bill Russell as individuals. They are the standard against which all other rivalries must be judged.

Starting in 1959, when the Lakers were still in Minneapolis and Elgin Baylor was a rookie sensation, the Celtics and Lakers have met in the NBA Finals 11 times. It is the most frequent Finals pairing, by far.

A modern fan might be able to wrap his or her head around that, but Wilt vs. Russ is another matter. Those two played each other 142 times over the 10-year period of their NBA career overlap (1959-69), and that's not even counting the exhibitions whose results are lost in space somewhere.

Larry Bird and Magic Johnson met each other 37 times as professionals, not counting exhibitions.

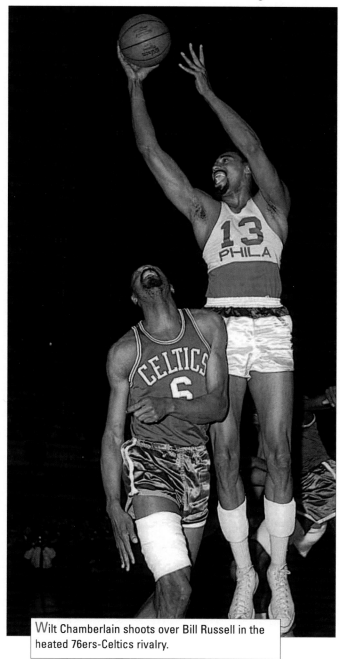

Wilt Chamberlain shoots over Bill Russell in the heated 76ers-Celtics rivalry.

There is a subtlety to a rivalry. Did meeting in both the 1952 and 1953 Finals make the Minneapolis Lakers and New York Knicks certified rivals? Perhaps. But the Lakers then, as now, were *everyone's* rivals as near-perennial champs, winning it all in 1949, 1950, 1952, 1953, and 1954. They were modern professional basketball's first legitimate dynasty. The entire league wanted a piece of them, but no one could compete with their great front line of George Mikan, Jim Pollard, and Vern Mikklesen, and there were few guards as good as Slater Martin.

The first great short-term rivalry in the NBA might very well have been the Celtics and St. Louis Hawks. They met for the title in 1957, 1958, 1960, and 1961, and the principals remained, well, the principals. The Celtics were built around the incomparable Bill Russell, who was abetted by such greats as Bob Cousy, Bill Sharman, and Tom Heinsohn. The Hawks were built around the great forward Bob Pettit, who was abetted throughout by Cliff Hagan, a rugged 6'4" forward who was death in the low post.

The Celtics won their first-ever championship in 1957, needing seven grueling games. It remains the only NBA Finals beginning and ending with double overtime games, the opener won by St. Louis and the final won by the Celtics, each, amazingly, by the same 125-123 score. A year later the Hawks won a finals re-match with Pettit scoring 50 in the deciding Game 6. To this day, Celtics' fans love to point out to anyone who will listen that Russell had a badly sprained ankle at the time.

Anyway, the Celtics prevailed in both 1960 (seven) and 1961 (four), after which the rivalry dissipated.

But a new one had already taken root. It was Boston-Philadelphia, and it had two phases. The first was when Philadelphia was owned by the venerable Eddie Gottlieb, a BAA/NBA original known universally as "The Mogul," and the second was when the Syracuse Nationals re-located to Philadelphia in 1963 and were re-born as the Philadelphia 76ers. Wilt Chamberlain was a vital part of both franchises, which only spices the plot.

Syracuse-Boston was actually quite an understated rivalry. The two met in the playoffs in 1953, 1954, 1955, 1956, 1957, and, finally, in 1959, when they staged a tremendous series culminating in a riveting Game 7, which the Celtics pulled out by a 130-125 score. The Nats offered such great players as Dolph Schayes, Johnny Kerr, George Yardley, Larry Costello, and, in that final year, Hal Greer, but in terms of it being remembered as a truly great rivalry, the spark never materialized into a roaring conflagration. A true rivalry needs something more.

A Wilt Chamberlain, for example.

By the luck of the draw, the Celtics and Philadelphia Warriors had only one playoff confrontation in the 1950s (1958). The Warriors were pretty much just another foe until 1959, when they unveiled a 7-foot rookie sensation by the name of Wilt Chamberlain. His battles with Bill Russell immediately became a monumental sub-plot, but the larger picture was even more important. For Wilt made Philly a winner, and the two had fierce playoff battles in both 1960 (Boston in six) and 1962 (Boston in seven). Beyond Wilt and Russ, it was Tom Heinsohn vs. the sharp shooting Paul Arizin or the menacing Tom Meschery; Bill Sharman, plus Sam Jones vs.

Greer; and, tantalizingly, Cousy vs. the flashy Guy Rodgers.

But there was more. There was the Boston Garden vs. the creaky Convention Hall (a building so intimate that a man could jump out of the balcony without even breaking a leg) and there was inimitable Celtics' play-by-play announcer Johnny Most, nightly denouncing equally inimitable Philadelphia PA announcer Dave Zinkoff, whom he loved to refer to as "Hysterical Harry" for his bombastic announcing style. And there was always Red Auerbach, taking on the Philly coach, whether it was Neil Johnston or the dapper Frank McGuire, the one-and-done Warriors' coach who indulged

Frank McGuire

Jerry West

Wilt to the tune of a record 50.4 points per game in 1961-62.

Given all this, Philadelphia was a true Boston rival, and it was all transferable when the 76ers came into being, all the more so when Wilt was traded from San Francisco to Philadelphia midway through the 1964-65 season.

Warriors, 76ers, it didn't matter to the Boston fans. The other team was wearing Philadelphia uniforms and they were the Bad Guys.

And, of course, the entire league hated Boston. Well, Auerbach, anyway. They all feared Russell, who was the center of everything on the court, but no one was neutral on the subject of Arnold "Red" Auerbach, who was a bad loser and worse winner in the eyes of America. Not that he did much losing once Russell showed up.

Each spring, of course, there seemed to be a meeting with the Lakers. Led by their great 1-2 punch of Baylor and Jerry West, the Lakers emerged from the Western Conference to play the Celtics for the championship in 1962, 1963, 1965, 1966, 1968, and 1969, the Celtics winning all six times.

For the Lakers, there were two great coulda/shoulda/wouldas. They were in 1962, when they could have won a Boston Garden Game 7 in regulation had Frank Selvy made a 15-foot jump shot (his specialty) at the buzzer, and in 1969, when Chamberlain's presence was thought to inspire a title against the very aged Celtics, who had finished the regular season with the worst record of the Russell era (48-34).

But the Celtics prevailed in that 1962 Game 7 overtime as Russell finished with 30 points and

Larry Bird fires a jumper over the rival Lakers.

40 rebounds and the Celtics prevailed, as well, in 1969, when Chamberlain was embroiled in a fourth quarter spat with coach Butch van Breda Kolff and Don Nelson clinched the game with a lucky, high-bouncing final Celtics' basket.

What made this a great rivalry was more than just the basketball. For here was a perceived culture clash between staid, tradition-bound Boston and the glamour of L.A. and Hollywood. The Lakers were the first NBA franchise to trumpet the presence of celebrities at a game, a practice which made Bostonians snicker. To Celtics' fans, the Lakers were laughable wannabes. To L.A. fans, the Celtics were fuddy-duddies who were lucky they had Russell.

Fast forward to 1982 and the "Beat L.A.!" chant. The teams hadn't played post-season ball in 13 years. But the Lakers had won championships in 1972 and 1980 and the Boston fans didn't like that. Elgin, Jerry, and Wilt were long gone, but the antipathy for Kareem Abdul-Jabbar (a rival from his Milwaukee days) and Larry Bird alter ego Magic Johnson was real. In the Big Picture, nothing had changed.

In the interim, the Celtics had developed yet another rival, one that was always ready to explode if only the party of the second part could ever develop a team good enough to hate. That team was, of course, the New York Knicks.

Geographically and culturally, Boston and New York are historic rivals in every way (ever heard of the Red Sox and Yankees?). But when New York was up in the early '50s, the Celtics were pretty blah. When Russell transformed the Celtics in 1956, the Knicks were down, and they would stay down for a dozen years, or until the 1968-69 season, when, buoyed by the acquisition of Dave DeBusschere from Detroit, the Knicks extended the Celtics to a tough six games in only their second playoff duel since 1955.

The Knicks ascended to the NBA throne in 1970. A resurgent Boston team gave them a challenge in 1972, but the veteran Knicks prevailed in an easy five. The Celtics won a franchise record 68 games the following year, but the Knicks beat them in seven games, becoming the first team to win a Game 7 in Boston. Playing without the injured John Havlicek (shoulder injury sustained in Game 3), the Celtics lost a painful double OT Game 4 to fall behind, 3-1, rallied to tie the series and then were completely overwhelmed at home in Game 7, 94-78.

By this time the rivalry was full-blown. It was replete with superb individual match-ups: Willis Reed-Dave Cowens,

Havlicek-Bill Bradley, DeBusschere-Paul Silas, Walt Frazier-Don Chaney, and Earl Monroe-Jo Jo White. There was the battle of the Two Reds; that is to say Auerbach, then Boston's general manager and very much still the face of the franchise, and Red Holzman, the Knicks' coach. Not surprisingly, the Two Reds did not like each other.

The games in Boston were particularly heated. In those days the Celtics could not sell out the Boston Garden on a regular basis, and when they played New York approximately a fourth to a third of the crowd was comprised of local college students with New York roots. You could call it a collegiate atmosphere.

Throw in the fact that the Celtics hated and resented the Knicks as an organization. Boston had the championship edge, but the Knicks had the money. The Knicks traveled by chartered flights when few others did. It was particularly galling to the Celtics when the two played in New York on a Saturday evening and then flew back up to Boston for a re-match on Sunday afternoon. Ah, those were the days, in every way – the Knicks would fly first class and the Celtics would fly coach.

Oh, this was a rivalry, all right.

But it wasn't New York's only rivalry. For starting in 1969 they had a real thing going with the Baltimore Bullets.

That one heated up fast in 1969, when the Knicks swept the Bullets in the first round, an achievement all the more notable because Baltimore had compiled the league's best regular season record. That was the first of six consecutive playoff

Danny Ainge of the Celtics guards Magic Johnson.

Magic Johnson, a Laker through and through, concealed a Boston shirt under his warm-ups as a joke on Larry Bird.

battles between the two. New York won five, losing only in 1971, when the Bullets stunned them in a Game 7 in Madison Square Garden.

Again, this one was chock-full of juicy individual confrontations: Reed-Wes Unseld, DeBusschere-Gus Johnson, Bradley-Jack Marin, Frazier-Monroe (until Earl the Pearl was traded to New York) and so on. The rootin'-tootin' Bullets preferred to run, run and run some more, while the Knicks were one of the savviest, patient half-court teams of modern times. As in all stylistic battles, the nightly winner would be the team that better imposed its will on the other.

The Celtics and Lakers resumed hostilities in 1984 after a 15-year playoff hiatus, and it was as if that 1969 Game 7 in L.A. was from the night

before. Now the point men were Larry Bird for the Celtics and Magic Johnson for the Lakers, but the star quality hardly stopped there. The Celtics also had future Hall of Famers Robert Parish and Kevin McHale, while the Lakers had future Hall of Famers Kareem Abdul-Jabbar and James Worthy.

Throw in luminaries such as Dennis Johnson, Danny Ainge and Scott Wedman for Boston, and Jamal Wilkes, Michael Cooper, and Byron Scott for the Lakers, and it was a classic confrontation, indeed.

The teams would meet for the title three times in four years, with the Celtics winning in 1984 and the Lakers prevailing in 1985 and 1987. The '85 victory was an enormous personal satisfaction for Abdul-Jabbar, then 38. He had lost to the

Celtics in 1974 as a Milwaukee Buck and again as a Laker in 1984, and he was fully aware of the history between the two. So it was a thrill for him to be the series MVP as the Lakers became the first team to clinch a championship in Boston. The second win over Boston two years later was almost anti-climactic.

All the old antagonisms between the two sets of fans were present the second time around. Now there were new, delicious components to the rivalry, such as the Bird-Magic debate and the presence of slick-haired Pat Riley as the L.A. mentor. The self-proclaimed maestro of "Showtime," Riley could not conceal his deep antipathy toward the Celtics as an organization, and the Boston fans were equally happy to demonize both Riley and his team. Each Boston-L.A. game, be it regular season or playoff, had a sizzle. The teams even had a brawl in a foolish-ly-conceived exhibition game. Players on both sides rightfully pointed out that enough was enough. Emotions were raw enough in the important games. No one needed to stoke the flames in October, too.

As the league's longest standing power, the Lakers have become a target for every team. There are many Western Conference teams who feel they have a legitimate rivalry with the Lakers, none more so than the Phoenix Suns, who have met the Lakers 10 times in the playoffs since their very first playoff appearance in 1970, and who won four of five battles from 1990 through 2007.

This is very much a geographic rivalry. The two are but an hour apart by plane. In addition, it was very much a personal thing for long-time Phoenix GM/Owner and even occasional coach Jerry Colangelo. He was in on the ground floor of the Phoenix operation from Day One in 1968, and the Lakers were the West's standard of excellence.

Another team that particularly enjoys getting a piece of the Lakers is San Antonio. The teams have met five times in the playoffs and the Spurs have won four, losing only in 2002. The Spurs have twice taken out the Lakers en-route to a championship.

Back East, meanwhile, it didn't take long for Boston to find itself with a serious rival after winning that 14th championship in 1984.

The Detroit Pistons had begun to take shape under Chuck Daly, extending the Celtics to an uncomfortable six games in 1985 and then really making them sweat in a frantic seven-game series two years later. Game 5 was the night of the famed Larry Bird steal of Isiah Thomas' in-bounds pass and subsequent feed to Dennis Johnson for the game-winning basket. Game 7 was a wild and crazy flight of basketball fancy in which Detroit players Vinnie Johnson and Adrian Dantley took each other out of the game early in the fourth quarter with a violent collision, Bird went off in the fourth quarter and the teams collaborated on a dazzling 36-34 fourth period before the Celtics pulled it out, 117-114.

Detroit upended the Celtics in six the following year, but it still wasn't over. The two met again in 1989 (Detroit in 3) and 1991 (Detroit in a bitter 6). There were personalities all over the place, with Bird, Parish, and McHale on one side and Thomas, Bill Laimbeer, and the immortal Vinnie Johnson on the other.

Robert Parish

And waiting their turn: Michael Jordan and the Chicago Bulls.

The Pistons and Bulls had first met in 1988, with Detroit winning in five games. A year later the Bulls thought they were ready after Jordan's famous buzzer-beater had taken out the Cleveland Cavaliers, but the Pistons had other ideas and won in six games.

Enough's enough, said the Bulls as the teams met for the third straight year in 1990. Chicago had heard enough about Detroit's so-called "Jordan Rules" as a defensive strategy, but the Bulls were sent home yet again in seven games.

A year later the Bulls really *were* ready.

They swept the Pistons and went on to win the first of three straight championships.

In recent years one of the most intense rivalries was between the Knicks and Miami Heat, a rivalry exacerbated by the fact that the Miami coach was Pat Riley, who had been the New York coach for four years (including a run to the 1994 Finals) before bolting to Miami, leaving only a fax message as a farewell. If his ex-players hadn't liked that, the New York fans had liked it even less.

The teams were fated to meet in the playoffs in 1997, 1998, 1999, and 2000, and what ferocious struggles they were. These were not games for either the faint of heart or the devotees of up-tempo basketball. By this time a completely re-invented Riley was very much into defense and physical play, and his New York counterpart, Jeff Van Gundy, was not exactly an exponent of Showtime, either. Each series went the distance (three 5s and a 7), with Miami winning the first and New York the last three. Perhaps all anyone needs to know about the way these games were played is that there were 22 of them and only once, a 101-90 Miami victory in Game 7 of the 1997 series, did a team break 100 points. In the 2000 series the Knicks were the only team to reach 90.

This rivalry was so intense the coaches would even get into the act. With 1.4 seconds left in Game 4 of the 1998 series, and the Knicks leading by five, New York's Larry Johnson got into a tussle with Miami center Alonzo Mourning. Knicks' coach Jeff Van Gundy, a point guard-sized fellow, sprinted off the bench to, as he said, "protect" Johnson. But the best he could do was grab hold of the 6'10" Mourning's leg.

The next day every newspaper in the land had a photo of Van Gundy, looking like an overgrown Chihuahua, latched onto Mourning's leg.

Pretty hard not to call that a rivalry.

Border War: College Basketball's Fiercest Rivals?

By Blair Kerkhoff

As a rivalry, the "Border War" between Kansas and Missouri stands alone in history.

In the years leading up to the Civil War, blood spilled in the streets of Lawrence, Kansas, and on fields around Kansas City.

This was American terrorism, described by historians as some of the most savage and merciless fighting in our history.

These were the Jayhawkers from Kansas verses Bushwackers from Missouri. Their causes were rooted in the political fight over free states and slavery. And while Union and Confederate forces battled in the east, often far from home, Kansans and Missourians horrifically went after each other in their home towns.

Which is why the very idea of another college sports rivalry to compare to Kansas-Missouri is almost laughable.

North Carolina vs. Duke? Kentucky-Louisville? Those are merely games.

Kansas vs. Missouri started with Congressional Acts and was followed by the Thirteenth Amendment, the final act of abolishing slavery.

Not even Army-Navy runs that deep

To this day, people remember.

Some Missourians, following the lead of their old basketball coach Norm Stewart, won't spend a dime in Kansas.

And Kansans, at least those in the Kansas City area, delight in reminding their neighbors and co-workers how the level of excellence in basketball mostly travels a one-way street.

It doesn't matter that KU/MU on the hardwood isn't celebrated like others. Sports television networks don't pitch it for weeks. It doesn't get the Dick Vitale seal of approval. It doesn't need it.

Stewart said it best.

"The top of the intense fans maybe get a little carried away," he said. "They don't understand competitors compete during the game. And then it's over. Unless you lose."

Beyond its historical origins, Missouri-Kansas comes complete with colorful characters, legendary coaches, and virtuoso performances.

MU/KU dates to basketball's originator, Dr. James Naismith. The rivalry rejuvenated the career of Kansas' Phog Allen, elevated the status of Missouri's Stewart, who made beating the Jayhawks a mission, and carried on through coaches like Larry Brown, Roy Williams, Quin Snyder, Bill Self, and Mike Anderson.

An old football coach, Kansas' Don Fambrough, pulled no punches.

"I loathe, loathe, LOATHE those people," Coach Fam said of his neighbors to the east.

This is why it's called the Border War.

The State Line: A Demarcation of Loyalties

For a full Border War flavor, drive down U.S. Highway 69 in Kansas and back along U.S. Highway 71 in Missouri. Stop in the towns that were once battlegrounds and talk, as *The Kansas City Star* did in 2003, to the folks about Kansas-Missouri.

In J&W Sports Shop in Fort Scott, Kansas, you'll find the gear of Kansas, Kansas State, Pittsburg State, and just about any other team based in Kansas. The Missouri state border is a few miles to the east, but not one shirt or hat in the store has the Tigers logo.

"No need for it," said store owner Lisa Stephan. "That stuff doesn't sell over here."

Nevada, Missouri, is home to Bushwacker Museum and curator Patrick Brophy understands better than most the rivalry's historical ties.

"I guess you could say that choosing a team and the feeling it represents is kind of like warfare," he said. "Just far more harmless."

Kansas City is the rivalry's epicenter, which makes it one of the most unique hot spots in college sports. Fans must exist together, and it isn't easy.

"There are so many bragging rights in Kansas City," said KU Coach Bill Self. "Not too many metropolitan areas are divided in half like that. With Illinois-Missouri it's more like Chicago vs. St. Louis. With Kansas-Missouri it's Kansas City vs. Kansas City."

Self, like previous Kansas coaches, gets the full treatment from Missouri's rabid student fan group known as the "The Antlers." They pack the end zone at Mizzou Arena, dress in wigs and makeup, and if it stopped there they'd simply be a Midwest version of Duke's Cameron Crazies.

Did You Know?

1930: Professional leagues eliminate the double dribble.

1933: For the 1932-33 season, women's basketball changes all field goals back to 2 points each, and guarding a player is made legal for the first time.

1943: Wyoming's Kenny Sailors is credited with popularizing the jump shot.

1964: The NBA extends the width of the foul lane from 12 to 16 feet.

But The Antlers' harassment only begins with their cheers. They're good with phone numbers, especially those that originate in Kansas. They've called Jayhawks coaches throughout the night, and have held up huge banners of KU players' cell phone numbers for national television audiences.

The taunts start an hour before the game when Kansas players step on the floor for casual warm-ups, and that's often the best time because the arena is nearly empty and voices carry.

The Antlers once held up pictures of Jayhawks Coach Larry Brown and Libyan dictator and look-alike Moammar Gadhafi and asked "Which one's the terrorist?

Kansas can give it back. In 2003, when Missouri guard Ricky Clemons was accused of striking a female acquaintance, a Kansas coed showed up in heavy black make-up around her eye and wore a T-shirt that said: "Ricky's girlfriend."

In recent years, the Jayhawks student section has put together a huge facsimile of a famous mural depicting abolitionist John Brown, only this one has him holding the national championship trophy.

They bring it out only for the Tigers.

Heating Up

A rivalry this combustible is bound to get overheated.

In 1977, during a game in Lawrence, Stewart was shoved by a Kansas fan. This came after a brawl between Missouri's Jim Kennedy and the Jayhawks' Donnie Von Moore. Both benches emptied six minutes into the game.

Afterward, Stewart and Kansas Coach Ted Owens met with Big Eight commissioner Chuck Neinas. "He told us to stop acting like children," Stewart said.

No moment was more volatile than the one in 1951 involving Jayhawks center Clyde Lovellette and Missouri forward Win Wilfong.

The finals of the Big Seven Holiday Tournament came down to Tigers-Jayhawks and Kansas was on its way to victory when, after a Lovellette shot, he and Wilfong collided and Wilfong went to the floor.

What happened turned Municipal Auditorium in Kansas City into a powder keg.

Lovellette planted his size 14 shoe in Wilfong's stomach.

"He was like a gnat that bothered my eye," Lovellette said. "You swat them but they keep coming back. He had climbed on my back. I got a rebound and put it back in. Then I shook him off like a dog shakes water off his back. He fell to the ground on his back. I didn't know why I did it, but I did it.

"I mean to tell you the whole place started hollering and screaming. I never heard such discord. I think even the Kansas fans were after me."

The boos didn't let up during the postgame ceremony. Finally, Missouri coach Sparky Stalcup grabbed the microphone and took the high road. "The University of Missouri enjoys this rivalry with the University of Kansas. Doc Allen is a great coach." With that, tensions eased, and

Allen's relationship with his adversary changed. The coaches became friends and Allen later attended the wedding of Stalcup's daughter.

This is the same Missouri coach who only a few years earlier was having a discussion with the officials about a call in front of the Tigers bench only to have Allen come over and push him. Stalcup raised his fist as if to slug Allen, and to the sure disappointment of Missouri fans didn't follow through.

Stalcup wasn't the only Tiger that Allen warmed up to. He tried to recruit Stewart, from Shelbyville, Missouri, and often spoke in glowing terms of the all-sport athlete. No doubt Stewart picked up a trick or two from Allen from his playing days.

"They conveniently placed the band behind the visiting team's bench," Stewart recalled his first visit to the new Allen Field House in 1956. "It was so loud that you couldn't hear your coaches."

But it was better than the building it replaced, Hoch Auditorium.

"Once, at halftime we came into the locker room and somebody had raised the windows," Stewart recalled. "There was snow on the floor."

Oh, the Tigers were pelted with debris that day after they became the first team to defeat the Jayhawks in Allen Fieldhouse, just as Kansas ended the Tigers' era in Hearnes Arena with a victory. The teams always seemed to find a way to spoil each other's fun.

Bringing Out the Best

At the same time, Kansas-Missouri has brought out the best in each other.

In his final home game in 1972, Kansas forward Bud Stallworth set a Big Eight Conference record with 50 points against Mizzou.

> At halftime we came into the locker room and somebody had raised the windows. There was **snow** on the floor.
>
> — Norm Stewart

"Coach Stewart always told us no one player could beat his team, but on that night one did," said Gary Link, a sophomore guard who had the misfortune of drawing the defensive assignment on Stallworth much of the night.

In 1992, Missouri's Anthony Peeler was amazing in Lawrence, firing in 43 points. He scored 19 in the final 7-1/2 minutes.

"He was unconscious," said Kansas defensive specialist Alonzo Jamison. "He had the glare in his eye."

But for high stakes drama, nothing topped the 1997 meeting in Columbia. Kansas entered the game 22-0 and ranked No. 1. The Tigers could only be a spoiler. They were headed for a humdrum season.

Momentum swings marked the game, even the final seconds of the second overtime. With the score 94-94, Kansas guard Jacque Vaughn knocked the ball away from Tyron Lee and the Jayhawks would have the final opportunity.

But the ball bounded to Missouri's Corey Tate, who scooped it up and splashed in a 16-footer with 5.6 seconds remaining. The Jayhawks didn't get off a final shot and the biggest upset in the series history was in the books.

Tate's shot was voted by Missouri fans as the greatest in the history of the Hearnes arena.

But in the final game of the old building, Kansas broke Missouri's heart with a last-second triumph in 2004. David Padgett, playing his only season in a Kansas uniform, swished a baseline jumper with two seconds left for the victory.

"It is as difficult a loss as I've ever been associated with," MU Coach Quin Snyder said.

Maybe it only made up for some Missouri stingers. Mizzou won the final time it visited Hoch Auditorium in Lawrence in 1955, ending the Jayhawks' 33-game home floor winning streak.

Stewart got a last laugh in Lawrence when in his final season of 1999 Missouri, won in Allen.

"The best noise I heard in my career was the silence in Allen Field House," said Tigers guard Brian Grawer of the occasion.

If the Border War has a face, it's Stewart's. "Stormin Norman" made beating Kansas a mission, and his 33-41 career coaching record against the Jayhawks mark the most victories by one coach over Kansas.

Fans at Allen Field House loved to hate Stewart, and their chants of "Sit down, Norm!" often filled the building.

Four years after coaching his final game, Kansas fans got a final opportunity to point Stewart toward a chair (which had been stationed on the court inside Allen Field House). Then-Kansas Coach Roy Williams paid homage to Stewart as a competitor and for championing Coaches vs. Cancer, a successful fund-raising effort that was founded not long after Stewart was diagnosed with colon cancer in 1989.

"I loved that chant," Stewart said.

But mostly, the series has belonged to Kansas. The first 261 meetings produced 167 victories by the Jayhawks, who measure their success in national championships, Final Four appearances and conference crowns, while their adversary hasn't been to a Final Four and its 2009 Big 12 Tournament title was the first for the program in its history.

The competitive imbalance is cited when downplaying the rivalry on a national level. And those who dismiss the Border War would be right, if only basketball and sports were involved.

History Lesson

To understand Kansas-Missouri is to know your American history. Take notes, there will be a quiz later.

With westward expansion, slavery became an explosive issue. The Missouri Compromise, enacted in 1820, allowed slavery in Missouri.

The Kansas-Nebraska Act of 1854 essentially repealed the Missouri Compromise and allowed settlers in those states to vote on the slavery issue. It was believed Nebraska would enter as a free state and Kansas as a slave state.

But free soil settlers began arriving from New England and the Midwest. Missourians from across the border were determined not to allow Kansas to enter the union as a non-slave state, but by 1855 free-soil settlers outnumbered the pro-slavery forces.

Big trouble started in 1856 when a posse of 800 Missourians traveled to Lawrence and destroyed the city's two newspaper buildings and burned a hotel. The "Sack of Lawrence" inspired abolition-ist John Brown to begin an eye-for-an-eye murder spree and "Bleeding Kansas" became part of the nation's vernacular.

Battles between Bushwackers and Jayhawks in small towns along the state line escalated after the Southern states seceded, and violence reached a crescendo on August 21, 1863.

William Quantrill, the son of an Ohio school teacher, learned that arrested wives and children of his guerrilla band had died in Kansas City when their building collapsed. He wanted revenge.

He led a raid into Lawrence and ordered his men to kill every man and boy they could find. Over the next three hours, 183 males were pulled from their homes and shot like animals in the street. It's been called the worst massacre of civilians in American history.

The raid horrified the nation.

"I have believed that the war along the Kansas and Missouri borders was more ferocious and uglier than any place in the United States because it got down to the individual level," said Civil War author Tom Rafiner of Parkville, Missouri. "This was the civil war."

The term "Jayhawker" became vile to Missourians. Most agree that the name, taken from a combination of blue jay and sparrow hawk, represented ruffians in the early years of the conflict.

But the name stuck to Kansans and became symbolic of patriots who worked to make the state slave-free. The First Kansas Cavalry in the Civil War was also known as the Mounted Kansas Jayhawk Regiment.

What would become Kansas' unique nickname meant something complete different in Missouri.

"I've read a lot of newspapers at the time that all refer to stealing and killing as jayhawking," Rafiner said. "When Kansas selected the Jayhawk moniker (in 1886), there were enough people alive in western Missouri who lived through those times. That name carried a lot of emotion, a gut-level dislike."

Missouri's nickname has roots in conflict. The Tiger was selected as the school's mascot in 1890 in honor of an armed guard of Columbia citizens who protected the town against plundering guerrilla bands. The guard was called "The Missouri Tigers."

War even reached the university president's office. Calling slavery a "God-given, natural right" in 1855, University of Missouri President James Shannon encouraged his students to invade Kansas and take on the abolitionists.

If he could have, Norm Stewart would have had Shannon sit on his bench.

The University of Missouri was founded in 1839, the University of Kansas in 1865. There must have been direct descendents of the border warriors sitting among the 3,000 at Kansas City's Exposition Park in 1891, when the Tigers and Jayhawks first met on a football field, and in 1907 when they first did battle on a basketball floor.

What is known from newspaper accounts in the earliest days is that the schools never liked each other and the rivalry's flames were stoked by some of the game's famed figures.

Phog Allen said that an important 1923 victory over the Tigers was the result of revenge for a Kansas football player, Tommy Johnson, who died after a hard tackle in a football game against Missouri some 15 years earlier.

Before the game, Allen pulled aside one of his best players, Tusten Ackerman, who had been a fan of Johnson's. Ackerman didn't know that the hit in the football game had only aggravated a kidney problem that Johnson had suffered as a boy.

"He told me, 'I thought they had done Tommy Johnson wrong,'" Ackerman said. "He said, 'Tonight, you're Tommy Johnson,' and he got me to believe it."

Ackerman scored more than half of Kansas' points that night in a big triumph.

Allen, who was a Missouri native, loved to take digs at MU, even in his retirement. In an interview just before he died in 1974, Allen explained

his choice of Kansas over Missouri when he enrolled as a student in 1905.

"I noticed that Lawrence had wide, paved streets," he said. "Columbia had muddy streets. They hadn't lifted Missouri from the mud then. The store fronts were different. Lawrence had all glass fronts and the merchants were very progressive in appearance, while Columbia had many of their store fronts boarded up. I could see the difference and I wanted to go to a place that was progressive."

In 1907, Missouri won the first two basketball meetings between the schools, leaving the game's inventor, James Naismith with a career 0-2 record against the Tigers.

Kansas won 30 of the next 32 meetings before Walter Meanwell, one of the game's first great coaches, arrived in Columbia from Wisconsin.

Meanwell was a native of Leeds, England, and had never played basketball. But he learned the game while working with slum children in Baltimore while earning a degree at the University of Maryland, and brought to Wisconsin a disciplined, ball-control style that nobody else was playing.

The result? Forty-four victories in 45 games. He left Wisconsin to serve in the U.S. Army as a doctor in World War I and became Missouri's coach in 1918.

Meanwell became Allen's target.

And Allen became the coach Mizzou loved to hate.

Then Stewart quarreled with Owens, Brown, and Williams.

Williams, a North Carolina guy, faced off against Snyder, the Dukie.

And Snyder bumped heads with Self, who soon found himself battling Mike Anderson.

In years to come other coaches will talk about the importance of the Border War. Other players will become heroes, and fans will taunt and tease. Just like any rivalry.

Except this isn't just any rivalry. This is history.

ICONS

"Icons" are the players, coaches, owners, officials, and others who have left an indelible imprint on the game.

A Dream Come True

By Mark Vancil

"Did I ever tell you about the dream?"

Looking around the palatial hotel suite with the ebony baby grand piano Michael Jordan would be playing in less than 48 hours, champagne in one hand and a cigar dangling from his lips, the answer didn't come as fast as another question.

"Wasn't it all a dream?"

By the time the Chicago Bulls embarked on the last leg of their second "three-peat," the road show had taken on the glow and passion of a rock and roll tour with the world's greatest band loaded onto the bus. Indeed, when the curtain came down for the last time in Utah in June 1998, even Pearl Jam's Eddie Vedder had a seat near the stage.

The face of the team was the face of professional sports, a leading man who had become a pop culture icon and whose influence extended across age, color, economics, nationality, and geography. From inner city 4-year-olds to white grandmothers in the Midwest to captains of industry, rock stars, actors, and the most imperial of political and world leaders, Michael Jordan had the kind of otherworldly magnetism unique to a production executed with as much style as substance.

When a team of NBA players visited a remote village in Africa in the mid 1990s, small children rushed into their makeshift homes to change into their best clothes. A half dozen emerged wearing sun-faded and torn Bulls t-shirts. On the other side of the world, NBA Commissioner David Stern was asked by then Chinese premier Li Peng if he would "bring the red oxen" to Tiananmen Square. In Russia, Mikhail Gorbachev wanted Jordan's Bulls to play in Moscow's Red Square. Thanks in part to technological advances in communications and television, no team in any sport at any time in history connected with so many across so many cultures at the same time. And at no time was the intensity of that connection greater than it was during the 1998 playoffs when the end came into full view.

It also represented the height of the remarkable career of a man who forever changed the economics of at least two industries – athletic footwear and sports marketing – while delivering one of the most complete and defining examples of excellence ever seen on any stage. It was a manic end-to-end effort performed with the grace of a ballet, the intensity of a world-class fight and an unflinching fearlessness.

But what made the mix so utterly remarkable was a single trait that had nothing to do with God-given physical gifts, marketing, personality or timing. It was Jordan's authenticity that lifted average teammates into champions and drove consumers to buy billions of dollars worth of Michael-related products. In the end, everyone knew at least one thing about Michael Jordan: He played for the love of the game and nothing more.

"I can't believe I've never told you about the dream," Jordan insisted.

The suite in the team's Salt Lake City hotel was similar to dozens of others once the championships started coming. The usual suspects attended to the usual game-day distractions, a movie on the television, cards on the dining room table, security that started at the lobby elevator and extended through the hallway and inside the suite itself. In a few moments Michael Jordan's pregame ritual, one he defined early in his career and refined as it progressed, unfolded in much the same manner as it had for 12 seasons. His custom made suit and shirt arrived from a morning pressing. The cufflinks and silk tie, selected prior to the trip for exactly this day, were laid out in the bedroom. The pregame meal that never varied, hot and protein-rich, arrived at precisely the moment it was expected.

Although the team could have walked from its hotel to the Delta Center, as Utah's arena was known at the time, the idea of wearing sweats for a five-minute bus ride never occurred to Jordan. If it's true that the first step toward mediocrity is doing what's convenient rather than what's demanded, then it's a step Michael Jordan never knew existed. By the time he boarded the team bus, no one could complain that the image didn't match the legend. Less than 30 minutes later, after he walked through a throng-filled lobby and then through another group waiting at the arena, Jordan was in the locker room preparing for the next routine. Years later, he explained the effort this way:

"I didn't want anyone who might be seeing Michael Jordan for the first time to wonder whether it's all real or just hype. I didn't want there to be any question about who I am or how I approached the game, on or off the court. I wanted them to know the whole show is real."

Actually, it was unreal from the first game of his first season in Chicago to the last game of his final season in Washington. By 1984 the NBA had been resurrected by an unlikely trio operating from the league's most important cities. With Larry Bird in Boston, Magic Johnson in Los Angeles, and Stern at the controls in New York, the NBA was rising. Although Jordan was expected to be an entertaining player in a long-suffering major market, expectations were muted by a number of cultural realities.

First, it was an era dominated by veterans. Bird and Johnson had earned their marks as rookies, but now they were the league's resident super-stars and one-time exceptions to the rookie status quo. Second, the Bulls were an under-achieving collection of high draft picks with more problems on and off the court, than success. Lastly, Jordan was considered a well-developed highlight reel with suspect shooting ability and a spindly frame. Portland had Clyde Drexler and thought it needed Sam Bowie more than it needed Jordan. Houston knew it needed Hakeem Olajuwon more than Jordan and chose accordingly in the 1984 Draft. As it turned out, neither of them won a championship as long as Jordan played an entire NBA season. In fact, Drexler didn't win a title until he joined

Olajuwon in Houston while Jordan was playing baseball.

What no one appreciated, however, was the nature and depth of Jordan's drive or the way it combined with circumstances that appeared aligned precisely for him. Spiritual teachers call this unusual confluence of seemingly random events "synchrodestiny." Despite all his obvious physical talents, Jordan's true gift was an innate ability to be cemented in the present moment no matter how chaotic the world around him. He had no fear because he was never anywhere but the moment he was in. He didn't look back and he didn't lean forward. Some people spend years sitting in an ashram in India trying to attain that level of peace and pres-ence. For Jordan, it was innate. Over the years writ-ers used dozens of words trying to explain the source of Jordan's impact – charis-ma, good looks, marketing, and simple timing among them. All of them were evidence of something more critical to the mix.

Stern showed up in Chicago for Jordan's third professional game. That night, October 29, 1984, proved to be the precursor of all that followed. In front of a crowd of just 9,356, Jordan scored 22 of his 37 points in the fourth quarter. He scored 20 of the team's final 26 points as the Bulls erased a seven-point fourth quarter deficit to beat Milwaukee 116-110.

"Why am I in Chicago?" said Stern. "The same reason everyone else is here. To see Michael Jordan."

* * *

Ultimately, all the numbers, accolades, championships, and awards add up to what might have been the greatest all-around individual performance in the history of professional team sports. There were an NBA record 10 scoring titles, a record-tying seven straight – broken only by his departure to play baseball at the height of his career - five MVPs, six Finals MVPs, a record nine First Team All-Defensive Team selections, a record 41.0 scoring average in the 1993 Finals against Phoenix, the 63 points against Bird and the Celtics in a seminal playoff performance inside Boston Garden, the 69 points against Cleveland, the "double nickel" 55-point assault on the New York Knicks in Madison Square Garden just weeks after leaving baseball and enough game-winning shots to defy expectation. He did it all despite missing substantial parts of two seasons and one entire season – 211 regular season games – all in his prime.

But there have always been great players with great numbers, and in the case of Jordan contemporaries Magic and Bird, great champions as well. In the span of little more than a single decade, Jordan went from being famously cut from the Laney High School varsity basketball team to being one of the most famous individuals on the planet.

So why Michael?

Maybe Phil Jackson's attempts to introduce Buddhist practices to his Chicago teams provide a clue. When Jackson conducted visualization exercises, taught players about the power of a "cleansing breath" and the importance of present-moment awareness, Michael understood.

"I had been doing some of those things my whole life," Jordan says. "I just didn't know there were names for it."

Though much can be made of how the planets appear to have aligned for Michael Jordan, it's likely they have lined up similarly for others. Only we don't know their names.

▸ When Michael was born in Brooklyn, New York, to Deloris and James Jordan, his mother knew the family had to move. The Jordans had three other children by the time Michael arrived. But this child, Deloris thought, cannot grow up here. Why? She just knew, that's all. Michael grew up the fourth of five children in the relatively bucolic surroundings of Wilmington, North Carolina.

▸ In retrospect, the family seemed perfectly assembled for a child of Jordan's gifts. He had a strong-willed and highly disciplined mother who worked in a bank and a charismatic father who had a military background and worked in a General Electric warehouse. It was a home built on fundamental values with little room for coddling and no room for softies or miscreants. "If you needed a pat on the back when I was growing up, then you better learn how to give yourself one," said Jordan. When he was suspended on the first day of his freshman year in high school, Michael became the first Jordan child to miss a day of school – *ever*. And when he tried to

A young Michael Jordan starred at North Carolina, which already had two established superstars in James Worthy and Sam Perkins.

scare his parents by threatening to run away, the act wasn't even acknowledged."I packed a suitcase and opened the second floor window," Jordan said. "I left the suitcase right by the open window so they would find it. Then I crawled under a bed that was near the window and fell asleep. When I woke up the window was closed and the suitcase was gone. I didn't hear anyone worrying about where I was."

▸ He wasn't a star until late in his high school career and thus had nothing but hunger when the time came to pick a college. Still, Jordan ended up at the University of North Carolina and in the care of Dean Smith in spite of his desires and those of his family. Michael wanted to go to UCLA; his family thought the Navel Academy or a smaller school would afford him more playing time. The former never offered a scholarship and Jordan declined the small schools because "a lot of NBA players came out of North Carolina." To say the least, his parents expected a college education, not a professional sports career.

▸ Smith proved to be the perfect coach for the raw talent Jordan possessed and the Tar Heels the perfect team. With two superstars and future NBA All-Stars in James Worthy and Sam Perkins, the team didn't need another star. Jordan could develop his game and learn from the low-key, team-oriented approach that defined Worthy and Perkins. "He taught me the game," says Jordan of Smith. In fact, Smith built the foundation upon which Jordan's adult life would later flourish.

▸ When the time came to leave North Carolina, the year was 1984 and the Olympic Games were headed for the glitter capital of the world: Los Angeles. Playing for the defiant and demanding Bob Knight, Jordan became the star of stars by leading the USA Men's Basketball team on a dominating run to the gold medal. Said George Raveling, one of the team's assistant coaches: "In two or three years, there will be a major controversy in the NBA. It will concern how Michael Jordan was allowed to be drafted only third instead of first or second." Leon Wood, a teammate on the USA team, said at the time, "I've talked with other athletes who've been watching some of our games. A lot of them are saying Michael is the best athlete they've seen here – in any sport, from any country. I tell them, `They ain't seen nothing yet.'" When it was over, Knight said Jordan might be as good as any player he had ever seen.

▸ Rather than being drafted by Houston or Portland, teams with the first two selections in the 1984 Draft, Jordan went to Chicago where his classic Midwest values fit the city's sensibilities and his competitive nature fit the team's need. Kevin Loughery who, like Smith, might have been the perfect coach at the perfect time, had Jordan for one season as the Bulls head coach. Loughery had coached a young Julius Erving and perhaps more than anyone in the NBA at the time, he knew exactly what he had in Jordan. Loughery effectively handed the ball to his rookie, and helped guide what might have been the greatest rookie season of all time, which is saying a lot in a league that had been transformed by the rookie performances of Bird and Johnson. Jordan lifted a perennially underachieving group of veterans into the playoffs by leading the team in virtually every statistical category, shooting better than 51% from the floor and 84% from the free throw line while averaging 28.2 points per game. But Loughery never failed to let Jordan know the points weren't enough if he gave up as many as he scored. Jordan hit his first game-winning shot as a professional in his eighth NBA

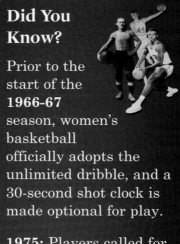

Did You Know?

Prior to the start of the **1966-67** season, women's basketball officially adopts the unlimited dribble, and a 30-second shot clock is made optional for play.

1975: Players called for fouls no longer are required by the NCAA to raise their hands for the 1974-75 season.

Prior to the start of the **1981-82** season, the NCAA adopts the Alternating Possession rule for men's games, jump balls now being used only to start games and overtime periods.

game. Said Loughery following the victory, "Statistics are misleading. I yelled at him a lot because he was playing poor defense most of the night."

▶ Along the way two other decisions fit into what might otherwise appear to have been a plan conceived by the gods. David Falk, a young agent with an immensely creative mind and an intense competitive nature that mirrored Jordan on both fronts, was selected to represent Michael. Falk grew up in the sports business working with and representing tennis stars such as Stan Smith and Arthur Ashe, among others, at ProServ in Washington, D.C. In Michael, Falk saw the future, the first player in a team sport that could be marketed as an individual. The whole notion of paying dues and waiting your turn, in Falk's mind, was outdated. Still, you had to look no further than Converse, the dominant men's basketball shoe company in the world at the time, to appreciate how far outside the box Falk was thinking. Converse had Bird, Magic, Erving, and dozens of other NBA stars. To Converse, the idea of giving a rookie his own shoe was not only out of the question, but preposterous. Meanwhile, Jordan wanted to sign with adidas and initially refused to attend the crucial meeting with Nike. In another twist of fate – for Converse, adidas and Nike – adidas never made an offer and Michael, at the demand of his parents, got on the plane to Portland. In less than a decade, Converse was bankrupt. Nike bought the company for $305 million in 2003, no doubt less than the value of Nike's Jordan Brand.

▶ Then there is his size. "In that sense, I guess I was the chosen one," wrote Michael in his visual autobiography, *For the Love of the Game.* "No one from my family is over 6 feet tall. Here I am, 6'6". Where did that come from? Why was I the one chosen to be over 6 feet, something totally out of character for my father and mother? You could go back generations and find one person maybe as tall as 6'2". But it's not enough that I'm bigger than the norm for my family. I have this special ability. I have an older brother, Larry, who has the same heart, the same kind of ability as I do, and yet he's only 5'8". This is a guy who would still play me one-on-one in a heartbeat. Despite all I've achieved in basketball, Larry believes he can win. Yet he never got the same opportunities. So I think about that now. Why me? I do believe my father knew. I believe he saw things unfolding in a way that no one, not me, not the Chicago Bulls, or anyone else saw. I believe that's a father's gift. I only wish I could talk to him now. How much of all this did he really see?"

About that dream . . .

"I knew the magnitude of the game, but I didn't fully comprehend what it meant," Michael said, sitting on a long couch in the Salt Lake City suite. At the time, the Bulls held a 3-2 lead in the best-of-seven 1998 Finals with the final two games in Utah. "It was 1982 and I was a freshman at North Carolina. We were playing for the national championship in the Louisiana Superdome. I remember riding to the arena. There I was about to fall asleep on the bus and I'm daydreaming about hitting a winning shot. I remember feeling so calm, so relaxed. I wasn't completely awake and I wasn't completely asleep. I was in a comfortable place somewhere in between. I envisioned being the hero in a game. I saw myself hitting the game-winning shot. I could see my teammates, James Worthy, Sam Perkins, Coach Smith.

"The dream wasn't game specific so I don't know whether it would be against Georgetown in a few hours or against another team in another year. But after we beat Georgetown for the championship, I told my father about the dream.

"He paused for a moment and said, `Son, your life will never be the same after that shot. Your life is going to change.'

"I thought, `Well, that's just my father talking.' Of course he's going to think that about his son. And besides, no one really knows one way or another."

* * *

Awareness

Jordan connected with the game the way he connected with anyone who saw him play. There always was something deeply spiritual about the depth of that connection. There were other players – Dominique Wilkins for example – who could jump as high or higher, move as quickly and score points in bunches. But neither Wilkins nor all the others ever came close to engendering such deep feelings with so many. In fact, it's possible no athlete ever has.

For Jordan, he operated in the here and now, in this moment and no other. That's why he could walk away from the game at the height of his career and plan it all more than a year in advance. To this day, his decision to leave

Michael Jordan

basketball after three straight championships and two gold medals at the height of his celebrity while risking abject failure for all the world to see might be the most remarkable sports story of the 20th century. It never occurred to him to consider failure, his legacy, or all the NBA records still left to be set or championships still left to be won. He was unlike an otherwise normal human being who would have been consumed with the future media response to an otherwise outrageous decision. In a society that had an increasingly unhealthy obsession with fame and fortune, Jordan went his own way on the advice of his own counsel.

Though the prevailing opinion is that the murder of Michael's father is what prompted his stunning decision to abandon basketball for his childhood passion of baseball, the fact is the entire plan had been constructed prior to the end of the 1992 NBA season.

The relentless climb to the top of the NBA combined with unprecedented marketing demands and a growing family at home had pushed Jordan to the limit. Still, there was no break on the horizon. Weeks after the Bulls dispatched Portland for a second straight title, the Dream Team started down the road to Barcelona for the 1992 summer Olympics. As bright as the lights had been to that point, the intensity of the glow was set to reach a whole new level for Jordan.

Once again, Jordan was the star of a star-studded team that included legends such as Bird, Magic and younger superstars like Charles Barkley, Karl Malone, and David Robinson. Outside of La Jolla, California on the campus of San Diego State, the Dream Team held a practice followed by player availability to media from around the world. When the practice ended and the doors opened to the media, Jordan walked deliberately through the crowd and into a stairwell.

With dark circles under his eyes and scratches up and down his arms, the remnants of another long playoff run, he slumped against the cold cement wall. We were alone, in that moment an ocean away with madness out on the floor.

"I'm going to shock the world," he said finally. "I'm going to quit and go play baseball."

It was July of 1992. As it turned out, the world would shock him first with the brutal murder of his father a little over a year later.

"The only reason I'm coming back next season (1992-1993) is because Larry and Magic never won three in a row. That would separate me from them. That's the only reason."

*   *   *

In different ways, each unique to the time, Jordan's last games, first in Chicago, then in Washington, epitomized the essence of the man.

The final 30 seconds of Game 6 of the 1998 NBA Finals provided the broad strokes of his entire career. Scoring when the only objective of the opposing team had to be stopping him from doing so. A brilliant defensive play when nothing else would do. A game-winning shot at a time when every player on the court had to know he was going to make the attempt.

The Score

With the Bulls trailing by three points, everyone knew Jordan would get the ball coming out of a timeout. In and of itself that was an incredible, though rarely acknowledged element to his game-ending heroics. It was one thing to think Jordan might ruin your night with a game-winning shot. Wasn't it an entirely different matter of simply keeping him from getting the ball in the first place? The Bulls had to score quickly to even have a chance against the Jazz. Jordan not only got the ball, but he drove straight to the basket and scored taking only seconds off the clock in the process. This against a Jerry Sloan coached team that seconds before was no doubt warned about precisely what had just happened.

The Steal

At the other end of the court, Jordan remembered something he saw earlier in the game. When Karl Malone held the ball looking to pass, he often dropped it down just to the right of his right leg. Jordan circled around toward the ball sneaking in behind Malone. Then he slapped the ball away. Even with all the points and high-flying acrobatics, Jordan never felt complete as a player until his defensive abilities were acknowledged. He headed upcourt as the sellout crowd rose to its feet in anticipation of what it feared was the inevitable.

The Winner

Byron Russell was alone at the top of the key when Jordan started to make his move to the right. As Russell bit on Jordan's break and flew by, Jordan gathered himself and started up into the air. He remembered thinking, "I've been short on the last couple shots. I have to follow through." Thus the iconic finish with Jordan's right hand waving the ball into the hole.

The Hall of Fame lineup of players Jordan personally kept from winning a championship was now complete. John Stockton and either Drexler or Reggie Miller occupied the backcourt. Charles Barkley and Malone the forward slots and Patrick Ewing at center. They all had to go through Jordan – Miller and Ewing in the Eastern Conference Finals – the rest in the championship round. Despite brilliant careers, none of them won a championship save for Drexler, who won at Houston in 1995, the year Jordan returned from baseball to the NBA with 17 regular season games remaining.

In Washington, Jordan's 40-year-old knees barely held together as the 2002-2003 season wound down. The kind of pain born of chronic tendinitis routinely stopped players nearly half his age, but Jordan played on. He played all 82 games, averaging 37 minutes. He shot free throws better and averaged more rebounds and assists than he did five years earlier in his final season with the Bulls during their sixth title run.

Though Jordan insists he is just one in a long line of players who over the years pass through the league and elevate the game, Falk, for one, isn't so sure. For one thing, no one has improved upon, much less reshaped, the sports marketing landscape Jordan created 25 years ago. Every great player gets a shoe deal; the best of them get their own shoe. There is a soft drink or energy drink deal, a fast food connection and others. Still, no one in any sport has yet to come close to creating what the Jordan Brand has become for Nike. Indeed, with sales of more than a half billion dollars you have to look to the world of high fashion to find comparable success built on the name of a single man or woman over such a long period of time.

As Falk wrote in his best-selling book, *The Bald Truth*:

"In hindsight, and I've said this many times, if you reverse engineered Michael Jordan down to the shot he hit to win the NCAA title as a freshman at North Carolina, being named Player of the Year in college basketball, his great parents, all the success in the Olympics, his work

John Wooden

ethic, smile and intelligence, it would still take a spark of lightening to ignite the mixture. The mixture alone wasn't enough.

"That's why in the 25 years between 1984 to 2009, every entity from the NBA marketing department, to the shoe companies to Madison Avenue have been like Ponce de Leon searching for the fountain of youth. Only in this case everyone has been looking for the next Jordan."

As Jordan heads into The Basketball's Hall of Fame, the search goes on.

"I can't say there isn't an ego boost or a higher sense of confidence in yourself when you have had as many lights shining on you as I've had," says Jordan. "But I never believed all the press clippings and I never found comfort in the spotlight. I don't know how you can and not lose your work ethic.

"Evolution knows no bounds. Unless they change the height of the basket or otherwise alter the dimensions of the game, there will be a player much greater than me ... I listened, I was aware of my success, but I never stopped trying to get better."

Just Call Him "Coach"

By Matt Fulks

Quick! Name the top five basketball coaches of all time at any level.

Plenty of names could be included among the five — Red Auerbach, Bob Knight, Pat Summitt,

Adolph Rupp, Phil Jackson. But one name *must* be among the top five: John Wooden.

To many, Wooden was a marvel. His numbers at UCLA during a 27-year coaching career are staggering. At the top of the list are 10 national championships during a 12-year stretch, including seven in a row from 1966-73. His teams won 38 consecutive NCAA tournament games.

Back-to-back UCLA teams, 1971-72 and 1972-73, went undefeated at 30-0. Oh, yeah, those 60 straight wins were part of an 88-game winning streak.

Chances are, not one of those records or streaks will be broken or even matched.

That said, though, Wooden wasn't the typical basketball coach. He was a sage, of sorts.

That description seemed to fit perfectly any time Wooden made an appearance, particularly away from his home in Southern California. During a Final Four weekend in Indianapolis, for instance, Wooden and his daughter were invited to a reception. They showed up without fanfare.

As his daughter helped him to his table in the dark and noisy ballroom, people stopped what they were doing and began to stare. They just watched him. They paused their conversations. They stopped adding chicken fingers to their plates. They halted feeble attempts at stabbing cubed cheese with toothpicks. It was as if they never had seen someone of his magnitude. In many ways, most of them had not.

After all, he was basketball royalty. His UCLA teams won more national championships than any other basketball team ever had or probably

ever will — especially under one coach. No, most of these folks never had seen someone of John Wooden's magnitude.

It was amusing to see the hordes of people who started lining up immediately next to Wooden's chair. They wanted to meet him, to have a photo taken with him, or to get him to sign anything from a sheet of paper to the back of a credit card receipt. By the way, this scene played out in 2000 … 25 years after Wooden retired from coaching.

It's as if there were something magical or healing just being in the presence of the "Wizard of Westwood." Wooden simply smiled and talked with people as if they were old friends. He graciously signed autographs or posed for photographs. He answered questions he's been asked thousands of times with genuine sincerity. He quoted poetry and passed along words of wisdom.

Frankly, he was himself.

Unlike other basketball coaches, great or otherwise, Wooden is a unique person on and off the court. There isn't one word in the English language that can describe Wooden. He's been called the "Wizard of Westwood." But he's quick to point out that he never has liked that nickname. You could call him legendary. That's accurate but not encompassing.

Actually, any single word to describe the man seems trite. The best word might simply be "coach."

In his world, that term "coach" meant everything good — father, mother, friend, teacher, counselor.

"A coach is a teacher first of all," Wooden said in 1995. "He must be a teacher and the teacher must be interested in not just the present but also the future of the youngsters who are under their supervision.

"One of the things of which I'm most proud of my 27 years at UCLA is the fact that all of my players graduated and practically all have done well in any variety of professions."

* * *

It's ironic that Wooden's UCLA teams dominated postseason play, and did so with the likes of many outstanding black players, such as Lucius Allen, Mike Warren, Henry Bibby, Sidney Wicks, Keith Wilkes, and, of course, Lew Alcindor. After all, Wooden is largely responsible for desegregation of national tournaments.

It's often overlooked that Wooden coached at Indiana State Teachers College before going to UCLA. Indiana State played in the NAIA (National Association of Intercollegiate Athletics), which has a proud basketball championship history going back to its days as the National Association of Intercollegiate Basketball (NAIB). In 1940, the NAIB gave small colleges

a chance to compete for a national basketball championship.

But, as with most national organizations at the time, the NAIA was segregated. The NAIA is less than proud of that fact today. Even the home for its tournament, Kansas City, was anything but desegregated at the time.

However, in 1948, eight years after the NAIB's first small-college national championship, according to the NAIA's website, "the NAIB became the first national organization to offer post-season opportunities to black student-athletes."

It didn't come easily by any stretch of the imagination.

In 1947, Indiana State, led by its first-year head coach, John Wooden, had one African-American player, Clarence Walker, a reserve.

In his rookie season as Indiana State's head coach, Wooden led the Sycamores to a record of 18-7. That was good enough to receive an invitation to play in the NAIA's national tournament in Kansas City. Since the NAIA was segregated, Wooden was told that the only way his team could play was if they left Walker behind.

> A coach is a **teacher** first of all. He must be interested in not just the present but also the future of the youngsters who are under their supervision.
>
> — John Wooden

Wooden refused to attend the tournament if Walker couldn't be with the team.

By avoiding the tournament, Wooden wasn't necessarily making a stand or forcing the NAIA's hand. To Wooden it was a matter of the team being together, making each player feel as if he were important in the big picture.

One great story displaying that attitude came from a time when the Sycamores were scheduled to fly to New York to play at Madison Square Garden. According to a story in Wooden's book, *Wooden on Leadership,* one of his players, Jim Powers, had been shot down in a B-24 during World War II. Because of that experience, Powers refused to fly.

"There's no way I'm getting on a plane," he told Wooden. "You can go without me, but I'm not flying."

Wooden decided the Sycamores weren't going to fly if one player couldn't or wouldn't. So, they gathered some station wagons and drove from Indiana to New York.

"It was family; nobody got left behind," Powers said years later. "His concern for us went way beyond basketball. We were part of a family."

That included Clarence Walker.

A year after Wooden turned his back on the NAIA, when Indiana State finished the 1948 season with a 27-7 mark, the Sycamores received another invitation to play in the national tournament. As the story goes, the NAIA decided to allow Walker to come to Kansas City. But, not wanting to make too big of a scene in the still-segregated Kansas City,

Walker was only part of the team on the court. He couldn't be seen in public with his teammates. And he couldn't stay in the same hotel with his team. Wooden, standing true to his principles even for a reserve player such as Walker, again turned down the NAIA's invitation.

The National Association for the Advancement of Colored People, however, didn't see the NAIA's invitation with limitations as a complete slap in the face. Instead, the NAACP saw it as a chance for a black player to break a national tournament's color barrier. Wooden finally acquiesced and allowed his team to travel to Kansas City for the tournament.

So, on March 8, 1948, Walker stepped onto the court at Municipal Auditorium, thus giving the NAIA the distinction of being the first integrated national tournament, and giving Wooden the distinction of being the coach who made it happen.

Incidentally, the Sycamores made a good showing at the tournament in 1948. They reached the championship game, but lost to Louisville, 82-70. Every member of Indiana State's team saw action during the tournament – including Clarence Walker.

Most of Wooden's philosophies and attitudes toward people, and his Midwestern home-spun goodness came from his childhood.

Growing up in rural Indiana, Wooden's family – parents Joshua and Roxie Anna, and four boys (the couple had two daughters, but one died at the age of 3 and the other at birth) – was not well off. In fact, the family lost its farm in 1924, when

John was 14. In spite of the struggles, though, Joshua Wooden stressed a positive attitude and Biblical philosophies to his children.

"Always try to learn from others, because you'll never know a thing that you didn't learn from somebody else," he'd preach, "even if it's what not to do."

And, "Johnny, don't try to be better than somebody else, but never cease trying to be the best you can be. You have control over that. The other you don't."

John Wooden carried his father's teaching with him throughout life. First, as an outstanding high school student and athlete. Then, as one of the country's best collegiate players in the early 1930s.

For three years at Purdue, 1930, '31 and '32, he was a First-Team All-America as selected then by the Helms Athletic Foundation. He was the Helms Foundation Player of the Year in 1932, the same year he led the Boilermakers to the national championship.

Wooden then went on to a successful professional career in the National Basketball League, where he was regarded as one of the league's best players. Fundamentally sound, Wooden handled the ball with great grace, scored when he needed to, and was a tenacious defender.

But Wooden wasn't concerned about being the original Michael or Kobe. He was drawn to education: specifically, teaching and coaching. He started at the high school level in Kentucky and later in Indiana.

Following his service in World War II, where he earned the rank of lieutenant in the Navy, Wooden started coaching at Indiana State Teachers College. He spent two years with the Sycamores before accepting the job at UCLA in 1948.

* * *

To say that John Wooden cared about the well-being of those around him and had an "Oh, my goodness!" Midwestern attitude isn't to say he was easy on his players. He demanded a lot and got more.

"Our practices were on a much higher level than the games," Lucius Allen, who played for Wooden during 1967-68, said in 2004. "We expected to win. We didn't expect anything less. It started with practices. Because of how hard we prepared, we knew at some point during the game the other team would make a break, but we felt we'd win. It was nothing for us to be down by 12 early in a game, but in the last few minutes of a half, the other team would collapse. We'd go back in the second half and keep the heavy pressure on teams. They had to play an up-tempo style of game. Teams would shoot 65 percent in the first half

Did You Know?

1939: Backboards are moved from 2 feet from the end line to 4 feet to allow more movement underneath the basket for the 1939-40 season.

1948: Rectangular glass backboards are made official for college play, and a new college rule allows coaches to speak with players during time-outs for the 1948-49 season (this was not allowed in women's games until the 1951-52 season).

against us and then 30 percent in the second half.

"But we never touched a basketball for the first two weeks of practice. Coach knew what we'd be doing through the course of a season. So, we'd go out and do cross country in the sand. When it came to the games, 40 minutes of full-court pressure was fun for us."

"I think some of the most successful coaches I know do not have a great winning percentage, but they come closer to getting maximum potential out of the youngsters they have under their supervision," Wooden said in 1995. "That determines your success; what you're able to get from those you have under your supervision. I don't believe there's such a thing as an over-achiever. We're all underachievers to different degrees, but no one does more than they're capable of doing."

> The best **pure** basketball that people can see today is among the better women's collegiate teams.
>
> — John Wooden

Although Wooden could be tough as a coach, most of his players left school with a respect and an admiration that has stuck with them through the years.

"(Coach Wooden's) effect has been most greatly felt in my attempts as a parent," Kareem Abdul-Jabbar (formerly Lew Alcindor) said for the book, *CBS Sports Presents: Stories from the Final Four.* "I've got to give Coach Wooden a lot of credit for what he taught me in terms of being a teacher instead of a coach. He showed me how to teach and challenge people without taking away their spirit."

"Coach Wooden had such an incredible effect on us, not just as basketball players, but as people," former center Bill Walton, who became one of college basketball's all-time greats under Wooden, said in 1999. "He really wasn't even a coach; he was a teacher.

"He was as inspirational and influential a person as I have ever met in my life. More so than anyone other than my mom and dad."

Wooden retired abruptly at the end of the 1975 season. He has maintained throughout the years afterward that he didn't realize until that final game — appropriately, a 92-85 win over Kentucky in the championship — that he was going to retire then. Again, "typical" John Wooden (if there is such a thing).

Despite his team's accomplishments on the court, Wooden's humble attitude remained. Of course, he'll take offense when someone talks about how it was easier for a team like UCLA to dominate college basketball "back then." What coach wouldn't take umbrage at that? (But, Wooden's reply to the statement might be right.)

"How many times had a team dominated in the NCAA tournament before our run?" he'd ask rhetorically, knowing another team hadn't come close to the feat of 10 championships in 12 seasons.

"If it was easier back then with fewer teams, then why hadn't it been done before us? I would say it is possible today, but it is not probable. There are things that make it more difficult now, such as players leaving school early. Some say it's more difficult now to dominate because of so many players leaving school earlier, but I say there are so many good players coming up now that the good teams that have a tradition are still going to get a lot of the good players out there. You don't see Kansas, North Carolina, Duke, UCLA and a number of the others ever lacking for material. They all have it. But, compare teams back in the 1960s and 1970s, there weren't as many good players. I think it's possible to dominate today, but still highly improbable."

Wooden has remained a tremendous ambassador for the game of basketball, regardless of the changes the game has gone through or will go through.

"We see tremendous individual athleticism, but we don't see as fine of fundamental play as we have in the past," Wooden said. "The dunk and the 3-point shot are spectacular, and bring enormous praise from the fans, but they have hurt the overall team play. Television has had a lot to do with that showmanship and individualism. I'd like to see a more fundamental game. If I want to see showmanship, I'll go watch the Globetrotters play.

"The best pure basketball that people can see today is among the better women's collegiate teams. They play below the rim and there isn't as much showmanship.

"Officials also are letting things slide as well which has changed the game. For instance, they are permitting too much physical play in the game. Dribblers now are allowed to carry the ball more often without being called. Traveling is seldom called. If a player is going into a dunk, he can nearly take as many steps as he wants. I've talked to officials about that who have said that the crowd loves it — particularly the pro officials with whom I have spoken.

"Those are the things about the game that concern me. But, basketball is still a beautiful game. It is still the best spectator sport of all because it is played with the largest object that is easier to watch. The fans are closer to the action — and it's a game of action."

Talking with Wooden has always been a treat and a blessing for anyone. Even for seasoned journalists. He's passionate about basketball. And he's passionate about life.

"So many people, as they go through life, develop levels of cynicism, bitterness, envy, and negative personality," Walton said. "There is not an ounce of any of that in Coach Wooden's life. It is a wonderful honor and privilege for me that I've had a chance to grow up with Coach Wooden."

John Wooden is a national treasure who should be celebrated. The Naismith Memorial Basketball Hall of Fame did just that — twice. The Hall inducted Wooden as a player in 1960 and as a coach in 1973. (He was the first person to be enshrined in both categories.) He should be honored not only for his accomplishments on the hardwood, but also for teaching us through his example.

"Coach Wooden is a pretty clever man," said Abdul-Jabbar. "He figured out how to take the two things that he valued most — family and basketball — to do his life's work and the Lord's work. That's not always easy but he pulled it off.

"There aren't a whole lot of people who can say that."

She Embodies Women's Basketball

By Mel Greenberg

Just a few years younger than the Naismith Memorial Basketball Hall of Fame itself, Anne Donovan has towered over the modern era of the women's game in more ways than her 6'8" frame, and she continues to add currency to her contributions as a player and a coach.

The Ridgewood, New Jersey, native grew up in a basketball family near New York City and went on to stardom in high school at Paramus Catholic, in college at Old Dominion University, and in the Olympics as part of two gold-medal winning teams with USA Basketball.

Then after Donovan's playing days ended, she went on to succeed in the coaching ranks, beginning as an assistant at her alma mater at ODU before serving a short stint as head coach at East Carolina.

She then moved to the pro ranks, guiding the Philadelphia Rage into contention before the American Basketball League's third season abruptly collapsed under bankruptcy.

However, Donovan went on to two-fold achievement. Professionally, she moved on to the WNBA, handling the expansion Indiana Fever on an interim basis in 2000 while Nell Fortner was guiding the Olympic team toward a gold medal in the Sydney Games in Australia.

She then moved to the Charlotte Sting and managed to pull one of the all-time in-season reversals in WNBA history as her team bounced back from a 1-11 start to finish runner-up to the Los Angeles Sparks for the 2001 championship.

Donovan then took the Seattle Storm to the WNBA title in 2004 and four playoff appearances overall. In the 2009 season, she became an assistant with the New York Liberty.

A member of the Naismith Class of 1995, Donovan translated her own Olympic experiences to the sidelines for USA Basketball. She was an assistant on the national team in 1997 and 1998 before assisting Naismith Hall of Famer Van Chancellor to the gold medal in the Athens Games in Greece in 2004.

In 2008, she was the head coach at the Beijing Games in China when the United States, loaded with WNBA players, overcame limited preparation time to dominate the games and defend its gold medal.

Donovan recalls when she knew basketball was going to be a major part of her life.

"The first significant time for me was in fifth grade," she said. "It was CYO basketball and it was the first individual MVP type trophy for me. It was time for me to realize not only was I tall but I had a chance to be good in this sport.

"The funny thing is if you go back to that time period, most of us didn't even dream we would be where we are right now," Donovan continued. "For me, the dreams revolved around the Olympics because I could see that growing up. But not professional basketball and the contracts players have overseas. It was not a thought. So it's pretty special to be where we are."

As a freshman at Old Dominion in 1980, Donovan, who became a three-time All-America, was part of one of the collegiate women's game's first twin-tower attack in the post as she worked with 6'5" Inge Nissen, a native of Denmark. That team also featured Naismith Hall of Famer Nancy Lieberman and was coached by former Immaculata star Marianne Stanley.

"Again, timing is everything," Donovan said as she related what it was like to be recruited when the modern era was still in its early stages. "And for me Title IX was just getting enacted. So, in 1977, I was the first in my family to benefit. I got lots of letters and lots of phone calls. But we visited five different schools at our own expense and

Old Dominion came to the forefront because of the prominence of their program and what intrigued me was Inge Nissen and I thought she was pretty fabulous and I knew I could learn a lot.

"When I went to Old Dominion, my intention was to study under Inge for a year – she was a senior and I was going to be a freshman and then emerge after that. But when I got to Old Dominion, there was an injury in the starting lineup so the whole process happened a lot faster than I thought."

By the time Donovan's collegiate career concluded in 1983, she finished as ODU's all-time leading scorer and rebounder with 2,719 points and 1,976 rebounds. Her 801 career blocked shots is still an NCAA record.

Her senior season also saw her named the collegiate player of the year. Donovan has also been lauded for her academics – she had a 3.5 GPA in leisure studies and was awarded an NCAA post-graduate scholarship.

Val Ackerman, who was the WNBA's first president and recently concluded a four-year term as the first female president of USA Basketball, has intersected with Donovan at various stages of Donovan's career.

"I played against her when I was at Virginia," said Ackerman, the

Did You Know?

1951: Men's college games are changed from two 20-minute halves to four 10-minute quarters for the 1951-52 season. This will be changed back in 1954.

The bonus free throw rule and 20-minute halves are officially adopted in women's basketball for the **1975-76** season.

The dunk is banned in NCAA games and pregame warmup drills prior to the start of the **1967-68** season.

recipient of the 2008 John Bunn award given by the Naismith Hall of Fame for contributions to basketball.

"She was awesome," Ackerman said. "There were not many 6'8" players and she was a great shot blocker. She could score. She was very dominating in the post and she was one of the reasons why they were a force."

"We had the misfortune to be in the same state so we had to go against her twice a year. So it was 0-2 for Virginia. But she is just a wonderful person. She is giving. She cares about the women's game. And has done anything and will continue to do anything to advance it," Ackerman said.

"She has been very instrumental in ushering the women's game into the modern era," Ackerman said. "When she played it was a very different proposition when she was at Old Dominion. There was no pro league. Women's collegiate basketball was not where it is today. And she has seen the game evolve and has been a key contributor during that critical evolution."

Donovan's best international moment as a player may have been in her final year in 1988 when after being relegated to the bench, she entered the Olympic championship game late with the outcome undecided. She made two key blocks and scored to help the U.S. win its second gold, but first in which a boycott wasn't involved by the former Soviet Union or the U.S. (A boycott had cost Donovan a shot at a gold medal in 1980.)

"She was that consummate team player," said Carol Callan, the women's team's national director for USA Basketball. "Consummate sportsman. She was that key player at that key moment to win a key game. It was an incredible tribute to her she could handle her role and then when called upon, could make sure that the plays happened."

Ironically, three inductees of the 2009 Class to the Women's Basketball Hall of Fame in Knoxville, Tennessee, all had interactions with Donovan either as a player or as a coach.

Cynthia Cooper-Dyke, currently head coach of Prairie View A&M who starred at Southern Cal and with the WNBA Houston Comets, was a USA Basketball teammate of Donovan's in the late 1980s.

"One thing I remember about Anne Donovan is she was a cool customer," Cooper-Dyke said. "Nothing ever got her too hot or too cold. And as a young player it was awesome to play with someone like that with that type of demeanor. She's a go-to player. She's a shot blocker. She's whatever you need to win championships. She was the first player that for her size had such finesse. She had such a way about her game that you just didn't see in the women's game at that time.

"I remember playing with her on the world championship team in '86 and one thing she wanted to do, she said, `I want to block (Uljana) Semjonova,' who at the time was a Russian 7-footer, and `I want to block her shot.'

`You don't want to win a championship?'

`I want to block her shot.'

"And we got in the game and we were playing well, and we were leading and Semjonova turns to throw her left elbow to hook and bam! Anne blocks that shot. She didn't go try to get the ball. She didn't try to get the rebound. She didn't try to save the ball. She was just like, `Yeah, I blocked Semjonova.'

"She was just a great player and great for women's basketball."

Donovan, who was inducted the same year as former Southern Cal star Cheryl Miller, spoke of defending Semjonova, who is a member of the Naismith Class of 1993. "I was the anchor on most teams I played on whether it was international or at Old Dominion, so when someone got past someone, there I was and I took great pride in that. Yeah, the basket was my house and the paint was my paint and I took great pride in protecting those spots."

Jennifer Azzi, a former Stanford and Olympic star, was coached by Donovan.

"The first time I played for her was in '98 with the national team and she was an assistant coach," Azzi remembered. "She was fantastic. She could totally relate. Obviously, she knows the game. But she could relate as a player and as a coach. I loved playing for her. She has done it all."

Former Louisiana Tech and Baylor coach Sonja Hogg coached against Donovan for Tech when the Louisiana school and Old Dominion were national rivals.

"My first meeting with Anne was when she played in the all-star game up at Kutcher's in the Catskills near New York City. I coached the South team and we ended up beating her North team.

"And I'm thinking, `She's going to have to get a little stronger' and suddenly, my goodness, she's going to Old Dominion," Hogg said.

"It was wonderful I could get to know her when she was a baby, at such an infant stage in her life and she went on to blossom, not only as a player, but her development just kept getting better and better. And then as a coach, that is the rewarding part to see these kids grow and mature as players and then take it to that next level.

"Annie will always go down as the sweetest. She was always special."

Donovan points to her international competition as a player and a coach as her highlight of highlights.

"I thank God for my career," Donovan said. "USA Basketball has been my life. It was who I was coming through the game. As a player, that's where I got my identity, so that's where my passion was: to be representing my country. It was great to have the opportunity to go through it as a player and then go through it as a (head) coach and against great odds.

"I know the rest of the world might not say that," Donovan said of the 2008 competition.

"But we were certainly at odds going in with little preparation, but tremendous talent. Don't get me wrong. I never underestimated the power of the talent we had. But with little preparation and the rest of the world catching up, I was so proud of the effort our team made."

And the game of women's basketball likewise is proud of what Donovan has brought to the sport.

The Night of 100 Points and the Dawn of a New Era

By Gary Pomerantz

At the moment of his great glory, a minute twenty-five to play, the kids in Hershey screaming, "Give it to Wilt! Give it to Wilt!" we see Wilt Chamberlain running the floor, a force of nature gathering power with each stride, and recognize him for what he is: unprecedented.

He came with an ego and a body perfectly sculpted for dominating his game. The ego was essential: For a player to score one hundred points in an NBA game, he must not only want to do it, he must, on a deeper level, need to do it – to take an opponent, an entire sport, and bend it to his will – to show that it could be done and only by him. In *one hundred* there was hubris but also a symbolic magic. In our culture the number connotes a century, a ripe old age, a perfect score on a test. Scoring one hundred points meant infinitely more than scoring, say, 97. One hundred was a monument.

Writers and players and coaches prophesied such a night for the young Wilt Chamberlain. He was a one-man revolution. He entered what was still largely a white man's game, took it above the rim, and made it his. The game's traditionalists, seeing the future, blanched. He was, at the core, an individualist, the ultimate alpha male. He loved the sport, he loved his women, and he loved himself. He was averaging fifty points per game during that 1961-62 season, and as his scoring numbers grew so did the prophecy. Pity the average NBA center of the day: several inches smaller, not nearly as agile or strong or well-conditioned, they became, against Chamberlain, desperate underdogs, some even sassing him by calling him "Globetrotter." Chamberlain luxuriated in the prophecy and admitted coyly that if he kept his cool, made his shots, then, yes, one hundred points was possible.

His body was a spectacle unto itself, like "a first sight of the New York skyline," according to one writer. Perfectly proportioned, seen from up close or afar, Chamberlain presented a physical majesty. He topped out at seven-foot-one and one-sixteenth and weighed 260 pounds, his upper body tightly coiled, not yet pumped up by the weightlifter's mass of later years. His broad back sloped downward gently to a dancer's 31-inch waist. "The most perfect instrument ever made by God to play basketball," the veteran Dolph Schayes would say. So long were Chamberlain's legs, he wore kneepads high on shins, in part to hide scars from thousands of mosquito bites he suffered as a kid on visits to a farm his uncle worked in Virginia near the Rappahannock; he used rubber bands to hold those socks in place and, in a quirky habit dating to boyhood, still wore a spare rubber band on each wrist.

His father stood a touch over five-foot-eight and his mother just over five-foot-nine. He heard stories about a great-grandfather six-foot-ten or seven-foot-two but he half-wondered if the man existed. To call him Wilt the Stilt meant you were not his friend. He hated that name. It reminded him of a big crane standing in a pool of water. He preferred the Big Dipper. His family and all of west Philly called him Dippy either because of his "dip shot" dunk or because he dipped beneath doorways or because Philadelphia had its share of guys named Dippy – there was Dippy Carosi, Dippy Chamberlain, Dippy this, Dippy that. Nicknames were the rage in Philly then, with asphalt stars knows as Tee, Misty, The Bird, and Hal "King" Lear. It's the same city that in the early Fifties sized up the Asian eyes of a high school basketball star Ray Scott and called him Chink – Chink Scott.

In spring 1962, professional sports in America, like the nation itself, stood at the river's edge, the waters beginning to rise and churn. The Fifties had seen Connie Mack, the "Tall Tactician," born during the Civil War, managing the Philadelphia A's in the Shibe Park dugout for the last time wearing his three-piece suit, necktie, detachable collar, and derby or straw skimmer. The Fifties had seen the NBA in its bumbling adolescence, the stepchild of the college game, virtually unloved and unwatched, with crowds so small (the joke went) the public address announcers introduced the players and then the fans. In those early years, it was a rough game played by military veterans and other assorted rogues rebounding with their elbows out, so rough that some NBA dressing rooms kept boxes in which players deposited their false teeth before they went out to play. Players smoked cigarettes (even at halftime) and washed their own uniforms in hotel room sinks (or sometimes did not). The game was that raw and run on a shoestring. One night, a young general manager, Marty Blake, lugged onto a train to Chicago two heavy boxes called "twenty-four-second clocks," mechanical devices used to time the length of each possession in a game. Blake served as public address announcer and official scorer for an exhibition doubleheader that night between the Minneapolis Lakers and Philadelphia Warriors. When someone forgot to bring basketballs, Blake scrounged around and found two for pregame warm-ups, one for the Lakers, one for the Warriors. As the game neared conclusion, Blake received bad news: the Harlem Globetrotters' plane could not land due to bad weather. This was a big problem. The Globetrotters were supposed to play the second game of the doubleheader. They were the main event. Blake called a timeout to stall. No use. He called a cab, two men grabbed the twenty-four-second clock, and when the game ended, Blake stood by the

Did You Know?

1979: The NBA adopts the 3-point field goal (23'9" from the basket); Chris Ford of the Boston Celtics makes the first official three-pointer.

The NCAA adopts the 45-second shot clock and the intentional foul rule for the **1985-86** men's season.

1952: The 1-and-1 free throw rule is adopted by the NCAA for the 1952-53 season.

Wilt Chamberlain during his days at Kansas.

arena's side door and announced, "Ladies and gentlemen, because of inclement weather, the Globetrotters' plane can't land. The second game has been cancelled." Blake broke through the side door to leave before the riot.

Into this carnival that passed for professional basketball, into the NBA's search for itself, strode Wilt Chamberlain. For the Warriors owner, a nickel-and-dime Barnum named Eddie Gottlieb, here, at last, was a must-see main act. In the old days in Philly, Gotty had scheduled and promoted any team wearing spikes or sneakers – up to 500 semipro baseball games a week – the 2nd Ward Republican Club, the All-American Thespian League featuring baseball teams like

the House of David and the Zulu Jungle Giants. It wasn't just that Wilt Chamberlain was a scoring champion. Gotty had had plenty of those: Joe Fulks, Neil Johnston, and Paul Arizin had each twice led the league. More than scoring, the Dipper added aesthetic value with his athletic grace and beauty. He moved with a dancer's elegance but at a higher plane. Gotty paid him $75,000 for the season, three times the amount he had paid for the entire franchise ten years earlier. He knew it would be a lovely relationship, an Old World Jew and a Philadelphia Negro, showmen both. The Dipper would score, stun, awe, win. People would talk. They'd pay to see him. They'd tell friends. Their friends would come, too. Gotty would win titles, help grow the young pro league. He would make a killing.

You had to stare at the Dipper, even if you were Red Auerbach. The Boston Celtics coach, a son of a Brooklyn dry cleaner, had seen Mikan and coached Russell, but even he, the great Auerbach, couldn't help himself the first time he saw Chamberlain, then in high school. Auerbach just stood and watched the Dipper walk. *Incredible*, he thought.

And so with a minute twenty-five to play on a winter night in a nowhere town made famous not by basketball but by chocolate, there unfolded a spectacle, a mesmerizing show of power, cigarette smoke, and a little Borscht Belt kitsch – the P.A. announcer Dave Zinkoff handing out free salamis and cigars.

Here came the Philadelphia Warriors guard York Larese, son of an immigrant tinsmith from northern Italy, leading the fast break. Larese took the ball to the middle, a teammate angling on either side of him, three Warriors moving toward the New York Knickerbockers basket, perfectly choreographed.

But from behind, covering ninety-four feet in twelve strides, Chamberlain was coming, and Larese felt the force. The local kids had left their seats in the Hershey Sports Arena by now, and they pressed close to the court and shouted, "Give it to Wilt! Give it to Wilt!"

From the Warriors bench, Coach Frank McGuire, a dandy from the Irish side of Greenwich Village, called out those same words. The tinsmith's son cradled the ball in his right hand and drove toward the basket, Knicks converging on him

from all sides. At the last moment, Larese lifted the ball high – a lob pass to Chamberlain.

Larese's momentum carried him beneath the basket and beyond the baseline and, as he drifted from the play, he looked back, and what he saw was unforgettable … beautiful and monstrous, exquisite and terrifying, a hugeness unlike anything he'd ever seen on a basketball court, rising up, up, up, Chamberlain, long and lean, leaping with both arms extended above his head, revealing the "PHILA 13" across his white jersey, catching the ball twelve-and-a-half or thirteen feet above the hardwood floor – two-and-a-half or three feet above the flimsy rim – and in one motion, slamming it through the basket with a ferocity that branded itself in Larese's memory.

The ball bounced high off the floor, and the Zink called out on the public address system, "That's nine-tee eigghhhttt!"

It's impossible to know in sports when or where the unforgettable moment will happen. That's the beauty of it. It can be a place or a time. It can be a personality or a startling achievement.

We remember Babe Ruth's "called shot" in the 1932 World Series in Chicago because of the sheer force of the Babe's personality – not to mention the bluster and the arrogance of the act – and because, in the darkness of the Depression, America needed heroes. Never mind that we still can't be certain if the Babe really pointed to the center field bleachers in Wrigley Field to show the hecklers in the Cubs dugout where he intended to hit his home run.

We remember Jesse Owens's performance in the 1936 Berlin Olympics because of its social and political significance. Owens, an African-American sprinter and jumper, won four gold medals to challenge the racial notions of the Aryan supremacist watching that day from a box seat – Adolf Hitler.

Beyond its Chocolate Town charm, Chamberlain's hundred-point game carried deeper import. Shot like a flare into the sky, it signaled that the pro game had changed in both the way it would be played and the men who would play it. It would be a game with a higher metabolism performed now at a greater speed, from in close and above the rim, by players who were no longer bound by gravity. The Dipper proved irrefutably that you could be a remarkable athlete even if you were seven feet tall or taller. Athletes had long been taught to be quiet and humble. Not the Dipper. He was fast becoming the most striking symbol of basketball's new age of self-expression and egotism – a development slightly ahead of the overall popular culture – and his hundred-point game gave him an imprimatur to continue being, boldly and unashamedly, the Dipper.

Chamberlain's hundred-point game carried deeper import.

His hundred-point game was also a hyperbolic announcement of the ascendancy of the black superstar in professional basketball. A wave of black athletes had been achieving superstardom in other professional sports for more than a decade: Jackie Robinson had cleared the baseball path for Willie Mays, Henry Aaron, and others. Jim Brown was annihilating pro football's top defenses, while the young heavyweight Cassius Clay, with his father proclaiming, "He's the next Joe Louis!" set his sights, eight months hence, on Archie Moore and then later *the big ugly bear*, Sonny Liston. In 1958-59, the year before the Dipper had broken into the league, Elgin Baylor rated as the only black player among the NBA's top ten scorers; now there were five scoring leaders who were black, and soon there would be seven. The hundred-point game was a revolutionary act – if not by intention then by effect – that announced the NBA as a white man's enclave no more. Against the Knickerbockers in Hershey, the Dipper symbolically blew to smithereens the NBA owners' arbitrary quota that limited the number of black players, a tacit understanding that was systemic in America (the joke among NBA writers was, "You can start only one black player at home, two on the road, and three if you need to win").

At the time of his hundred-point game, Chamberlain was 25 years old, still in the process of *becoming*, though already at the height of his considerable athletic powers. His standing reach was nine feet, seven inches, his arm span eighty-nine inches. He'd run the 440 in forty-nine seconds, leaped nearly twenty-three feet in the broad jump, and put the shot more than fifty-three feet. He could clean and jerk 375 pounds and dead-lift 625 pounds. If athleticism may be defined exclusively as a combination of size, strength, speed, and agility, then the young Wilt Chamberlain, at seven-foot-one, 260 pounds, might have been the twentieth century's greatest pure athlete. He would transform his sport, and its geometry, more than anyone ever did: he led the movement that took a horizontal game and made it vertical.

Already, he was a celebrated individualist, a bachelor with enormous cravings, an intergalactic nickname, and all the trappings of new money. He had a fancy car, a racehorse (Spooky Cadet), apartments on both coasts, and a famous Harlem nightclub – where Malcolm X had served as a teenaged waiter – that now bore the name Big Wilt's Small's Paradise. The Warriors' owner, Eddie Gottlieb, worked to keep Chamberlain happy. As part of their agreement, Gotty rented the Dipper a gorgeous three-bedroom apartment at the Hopkinson House, a prestigious new high-rise. It overlooked Independence Hall, where the Founding Fathers ratified America's defining documents, and was near the nation's first Executive Mansion where George and Martha Washington lived during the 1790s (with eight Negro slaves). There, the Dipper roomed with Vince Miller, whom he had known since third grade, his deepest and most enduring boyhood friendship. Miller was his teammate at Overbrook High and even before at Shoemaker Junior High where they wore red-white-and-blue socks pulled up nearly to the knees. That's when he began using rubber bands to keep them in place. The Dipper wore the spare rubber bands on his wrists throughout his NBA career to remind him of those early friendships, the ones that preceded the arrival of the groupies and sycophants.

In 1962, only its sixteenth season, the NBA struggled to compete with the more established college game, which had troubles of its own. Basketball had been damaged by the betting and point-shaving scandals in the colleges during the early Fifties; now, a decade later, a new college gambling scandal struck, twice the size of the first, involving at least fifty players from twenty-seven schools in nearly two dozen states. The NBA's failure to capture the American imagination showed in sparse crowds and small television ratings. The Warriors even played one game that season against the expansion Chicago Packers in a high school gymnasium in Indiana. NBA games could be physical, even violent. Fights broke out on the court. Penny-ante gamblers still worked the crowd in some NBA arenas. With only one team west of St. Louis, the NBA hardly seemed *national*. When the Lakers moved to Los Angeles in 1960 they found themselves virtual foreigners in a Pacific Coast League baseball town. The team dispatched players in sound trucks to Beverly Hills, Hollywood, and south central Los Angeles to give clinics and read from scripts: *"Hello, I'm*

Did You Know?

1983: The collegiate five-second closely guarded play is changed from a jump ball to a turnover for the 1982-83 NCAA season for men, and in the following season for women.

1992: For the 1992-93 NCAA season, unsportsmanlike technical fouls count toward a player's disqualification and a team's bonus situation.

1997: The NBA three-point line is lengthened to its original distance of 23'9" (except in the corners where it remains at 22').

Tommy Hawkins of the Los Angeles Lakers. We're going to be at the Sports Arena for the next ten days. First up: the New York Knicks on Friday. Please come out to see us." The Lakers' attendance wasn't helped when the U.S. Army called for Private Elgin Baylor. Stationed in Fort Lewis in Washington, Baylor missed nearly half the 1961-62 season, doing his best to obtain passes to play games on weekends. The NBA, in its rudimentary development and reach, was in 1962 roughly the equal of baseball at the dawn of the live-ball era in the early 1920s, an old era fading and a new one rising with exciting possibilities.

Occasionally NBA games were played in outlying towns like Hershey in an attempt to attract new fans. The Knicks and Warriors rosters on March 2, 1962, were a snapshot of American manhood at midcentury, filled with first-generation Americans carrying their fathers' Old World names (Meschery, Larese, Radovich) and former U.S. Marines (Arizin, Guerin, Green). Their childhoods had been shaped by the Depression and World War II when their fathers worked as cops, for the railroads, in coal mines, and as common laborers. The father of one of the Dipper's teammates in Hershey fought with the White Russians against the Bolsheviks after the October 1917 revolution.

Chamberlain's hundred-point game was played in a drafty old gym in Pennsylvania Dutch country, up the street from Milton Hershey's famous chocolate factory, spreading its sweet fumes.

No television cameras were there.

Neither was the New York press.

Only two photographers showed up; one left in the first quarter, the other took just a few pictures.

Only 4,124 people attended, leaving nearly 4,000 seats empty. Chamberlain's hundred-point game played out under the media radar and lives largely in the memory of those who played in it or watched it.

On the bus ride home through the Amish lands late that night, Chamberlain's teammates spotted a farmer driving his horse-drawn buggy by a lantern's light. Chamberlain never saw that. He was in a new Cadillac, no bus for him, cruising back to his nightclub in Harlem. Showered and tired but exhilarated from his night's work, he still had time to celebrate. Big Wilt's Small's Paradise didn't turn off its lantern lights until four in the morning.

CREDIT LINE: From WILT, 1962 by Gary M. Pomerantz, Copyright © 2005 by Gary M. Pomerantz. Used by permission of Crown Publishers, a division of Random House, Inc.

Bob Knight and the Basketball Hall of Fame Family Tree

By Bob Hammel

It's probably true to some degree for most of the distinguished honorees in there. Maybe, all of them. But surely only a few of them — only a few of the basketball giants immortalized with recognition in the Naismith Memorial Basketball Hall of Fame – walk among those plaques, mentally sifts through those names, and feels for so many the genuine warmth and appreciation that Bob Knight does. Bob Knight, a man rarely publicly identified with the words "warmth" and "appreciation."

Knight properly is known for winning. He did it more often than anyone else who ever coached in men's major-college basketball. He is known as a fierce competitor; properly so; known as an innovator, on offense and defense; as a tactician, who let his opponents know months and years in advance what he basically planned to do against them at both ends of the court and always, unfailingly, blended in just enough of a wrinkle here or there to make each game plan look, and feel, and truly be, tailored to achieve specific one-game goals.

Knight, in six years at Army and 29 at Indiana and six-plus at Texas Tech, did all that while insisting, like Solomon in Ecclesiastes, there really was nothing new under the sun – nothing being done by him or anyone in college basketball today that didn't have its roots in what the pioneers of the sport figured out as The Way To Play The Game long, long ago. That was appreciation, and warmth, whatever the public image.

Knight's least-acknowledged strength was as a listener.

Army's head coach at 24, Knight already had Fred Taylor (HOF 1986) as his mentor after Taylor, himself the third-youngest man ever to win an NCAA major-college basketball championship, had included him in one of the strongest recruiting classes in the history of the game. Jerry Lucas (HOF 1979) and John Havlicek (HOF 1983) were the headliners of that class. Havlicek became a close friend who always seemed to be there at peak moments through Knight's coaching career. Taylor coached Knight at Ohio State for four seasons, and sent him out to make his own coaching way, with lines of contact and support always maintained.

In his mid-20s, Knight established a link with St. John's legend Joe Lapchick (HOF 1966), and followed up with visits to Lapchick's home. Thirty, forty years later, Knight still knew the street and house number, and just about every word of advice Lapchick gave him on things like training rules, pursuit of popularity – a basic common-sense list Knight treasured and lived by. He also cherished a scrapbook Lapchick passed along to him after Lapchick's death: of clippings from the stunning days of the 1950s college basketball point-shaving scandal in New York, shown by Lapchick to every subsequent St. John's team he coached as a warning of the ever-present danger of contact with gamblers.

While still in his mid-20s, Knight formed an acquaintance, then a long-lasting friendship, with one of the sport's tiniest and wisest grand masters, Clair Bee (HOF 1967), whose second-degree burns from the ignominy and indignity of having players caught up in those scandals banished him into upstate New York oblivion – but in proximity to the hungry young mind building thoughts and plans at upstate West Point, New York.

Fred Taylor introduced Knight to a basketball-shrewd friend of his, Stu Inman. Inman and Taylor were Knight's bridge to a friend of theirs, Pete Newell (HOF 1978). When Knight met Newell, King Arthur had met Merlin. After that, minds attuned to building a more perfect game got together frequently every season Knight coached, to analyze every team, every player Knight ever had. When not together, telephones worked fine. So did films, then tapes shipped out by Knight to Newell in California for study and analysis, then suggestions and recommendations.

In 1972, when his Indiana program was barely launched and far from the orbit it soon achieved, Knight accepted an invitation to work under United States coach Henry Iba (HOF 1968) in the trials competition that selected the Olympic team Iba took to Munich. Out of that came another mentor-student relationship that eventually brought Iba to Bloomington annually for on-site critiques. In 1984, Knight made the long-retired Iba part of his own Olympic staff, and on gold medal night at Los Angeles, before Knight accepted a victory ride atop celebrating team members' shoulders, he forwarded Iba for the ride Knight always felt had been denied him 12 years before in the controversial loss to the Soviets at Munich. And, in the summer of 1985, when Knight expanded his Indiana team's invitation to an international tournament in Japan into a world-circling tour, both Iba and Everett Dean (HOF 1966) made the full 5-week trip – Iba at 81, Dean at 87, having the last great basketball adventure of their remarkable lives. Less apparent but true: each, in the months just before, had lost his wife. Knight never mentioned that to either in making what could

have been lonely months for them into upbeat reminders of life around a vibrant young basketball team.

Dean had been another whose warm counsel Knight sought out early in his IU days and always valued. Dean was the man Knight continually made sure was recognized as the father of Indiana University basketball: the first All-America player at a hitherto basketball non-entity, then the first coach to win a Big Ten championship there, the man who brought in the squad that Dean's own All-America star Branch McCracken (HOF 1960) coached to the school's first NCAA championship in 1940, and himself an NCAA-championship coach at Stanford in 1942. Everett Dean, Branch McCracken, Bob Knight: the three Rushmore faces of Indiana University basketball.

Knight's Hall of Fame reach extended farther. A friendship that began with an introduction through Havlicek developed into another rich listening opportunity for Knight with Red Auerbach (HOF 1968). Their spheres of operation were quite different; their game wasn't. Their dinners, lunches, phone conversations, and other times together seemed mutually prized.

Knight formed a contemporary friendship with his most frequent companion at the top of college basketball in the '70s and '80s, Dean Smith (HOF 1982). Their relationship was so close the two tried playing a home-and-home regular-season match-up but before the "series" could take on classic stature both preferred cutting it off so they felt freer to exchange tapes and comments on each other's current teams. It was

Smith whom Knight's 880th coaching victory finally moved him past, a pass of the baton that seemed to mean more to each because the other added legitimacy to the schmaltzy media-boomed title of All-Time Winningest Coach.

In his Indiana days when he didn't need to travel to fill a schedule and most programs of that stature didn't, Knight signed into a home-and-home link-up with far-off Texas-El Paso, because of his friendship with and admiration for the coaching style of Don Haskins (HOF 1997). Both learned things about their own teams from those matchups, and from off-season fishing trips by the two salty competitors. When Haskins died in September 2007, *Time Magazine*'s tribute column on him was written by Knight, who said: "There's a myth, perpetuated by the press and the 2006 Disney movie 'Glory Road,' that it took exceptional courage for Don to start an all-black team. Not really. It took a guy who didn't care about colors. He would have started five white kids or five Chinese kids if that gave him the best chance to win. Don's legacy is that he played the game the way he thought it should be played, without prejudice."

Knight recruited and coached, then brought in as an assistant, then sent out – as Taylor had him – Mike Krzyzewski (HOF 2001) to build his own epic coaching career. When Krzyzewski was inducted into the Hall, Knight was his presenter.

Another Knight recruit and player, Isiah Thomas (HOF 2000), won the Final Four's Most Outstanding Player Award in 1981 as the All-America leader of the middle of Knight's three NCAA champions at Indiana – before his

championship and All-NBA years with the Detroit Pistons.

Keeping track? What is that, 13 Hall of Famers bejeweling Bob Knight's coaching path? Not counting the 14th (Bob Knight: HOF 1991).

Bob Knight was always a shooter, always a scorer in four varsity years at Orrville High School in northeastern Ohio – Akron and Cleveland a little more north, football-famous Massillon just a little bit east, the Smucker's jelly factory in his own backyard. Knight did play football, as Buckeye athletes must – a two-way end and punter. He always felt later that baseball was the game that best suited his skills. But basketball took him to college and pointed him toward a career and fame.

It was to come not for his shooting or his scoring. For three years, he was primarily a leading substitute during a great era at Ohio State. Those were the years that introduced him to championships: Big Ten (the three Buckeye teams he played on won championships each year and in going 40-2 never lost a league game before their title was clinched), and NCAA (three tournament trips, all to the final game, winners in 1960, losers to state rival Cincinnati in '61 and '62). Those years showed him championships were not a Holy Grail, an Impossible Dream, but attainable and worthy of a commitment. They also represented gauges of how close each of his teams came to being as good as it could be – *that* team, not the one the year before or the year after, but that particular team, with its blend of strengths and shortcomings.

In the years when his Indiana teams were themselves the measuring stick for their Big Ten rivals, every Hoosier team began the season with a basic goal of winning the conference championship. If developments justified, the goal at regular season's end became reaching the Final Four. Once they got there, as five of his Indiana teams did, the goal moved up to winning the whole thing. And three did, as many as any contemporary did after retirements of first Adolph Rupp (four championships, HOF 1968), then John Wooden (with his unimaginable 10 championships and historic HOF double: 1960 for playing, 1973 for coaching). Even the Rupp and Wooden careers overlapped with Knight's. Rupp's last Kentucky team lost a 90-89 double-overtime game to Knight's first Indiana team, a game distinguished in Hoosier lore by Indiana center Steve Downing's 50-minute, 47-point, 25-rebound performance. Wooden's 1973 championship included a 70-59 semifinal victory over Knight's first Big Ten champion and Final Four team at Indiana, much more of a scare for the Bruins than the score sounds. A late-game block-charge call that went for UCLA All-America Bill Walton and against Downing was crucial in a game that, loss and all, signaled the legitimacy of the Knight program's arrival as a national factor.

Knight and Wooden almost got together earlier. A history major, Knight left Ohio State with law school thoughts. Taylor talked with Wooden about a graduate assistant job for Knight while he pursued graduate work. This was 1962; the military draft was alive. A possibility emerged for Knight to control his military obligation by joining the Army – his railroader father thought he was nuts to do that – with the understanding he would serve his two years as a graduate assistant coach at West Point under George Hunter, a friend of Taylor. Pat Knight thought his son was nuts for that part of the arrangement, too. "You don't go to college to be a coach – anyone can coach," the elder Knight reasoned. And then the son questioned his own sensibilities when, after enlisting and before leaving for West Point, he got a call from Taylor and heard that Hunter had been fired.

A young assistant only a few years older than Knight, Taylor "Tates" Locke, moved into Hunter's job, honored the commitment with Knight, and a new world opened to him. Locke's basketball philosophy was defense-based, cautious and possession-prizing above flash and dash on offense, and he brought Knight in on planning, on recruiting, on working with players pointed toward military careers, not athletic. Those two years under Locke, then six as Army's coach after Locke left for Miami of Ohio, were among Knight's favorites, though his greater fame and much greater success came later. Winning three national championships at Indiana didn't seem to mean a bit more to him than his Army teams going 6-0 against Navy. Playing in the National Invitation Tournament over the years took on an element of scorn for most of major-college basketball's elite, but winning the NIT with Indiana in 1979 was a genuine highlight moment for Knight, because competing in that tournament and pursuing that championship was such a grand and elusive goal in his Army days. "We've won – we've *won* the *NIT*!" he shouted on-court at Madison Square Garden that night, pure inside-out glee – which went undisplayed in the midst of post-game celebrations after his Indiana teams' three NCAA championships – reflective of his Army years and near-miss frustrations.

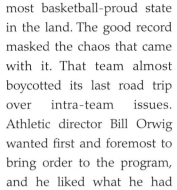

We've won! We've won the NIT!

— Bob Knight

The intelligent dedication that his Army teams gave to the basketball he taught were a shadow that his more talent-blessed teams at Indiana never really were able to come out from – maybe, *maybe* working up to similar stature in going unbeaten for two straight regular seasons at Indiana capped by the last perfect season a major-college men's team ever managed. That was in 1975-76, an "ever" that reached 30 years in 2006 and has kept aging since. And even that Indiana team, through its coach's eyes and words, saw those Army teams and players as supermen.

Knight went 102-50 in his six West Point years. But less his record than his growing reputation as a disciplinarian, and his identification with the no-nonsense, Big Ten-dominating Taylor, made the 30-year-old Knight Indiana's coach when its job opened in Spring 1971. That 1970-71 season had been Knight's only losing year at Army (11-13), and by record (17-7) Indiana's best in a

six-year stretch that had included four last-place Big Ten finishes for the representative of the most basketball-proud state in the land. The good record masked the chaos that came with it. That team almost boycotted its last road trip over intra-team issues. Athletic director Bill Orwig wanted first and foremost to bring order to the program, and he liked what he had heard about the brilliant basketball mind of the young disciplinarian he was bringing in.

Knight inherited one other challenge. Indiana in his first year opened its new basketball palace: Assembly Hall, with 17,200 plush seats to fill or be embarrassingly empty, after years of rarely coming close to filling a 10,000-seat fieldhouse. By his second year, Knight was filling it regularly; by his fourth, it was selling out with season tickets, and for subsequent decades getting on the list for buying those season tickets became envied status.

In truth, it's a lousy spectator arena. Almost a fourth of those seats are in a balcony, with a straight-down view from such a height that arched shots look like straight-line hockey passes – such a height that the first event in the building was Ringling Brothers Barnum & Bailey circus and balcony ticketholders looked down on the high-wire act. Even in the main-floor sections, seats go up at a sharp angle – up and up and up, which makes walking down feel a bit treacherous. But, when all those seats are filled on a game night, opponents look up into peopled walls of red, with all-around sound that the Dolby movie technologists at their best can't top. There are bigger, there are better college basketball arenas, but under Knight it took on such singular distinction that national columnist Dan Wetzel once wrote: "Face it, when you see a game from Assembly Hall come on TV, it just feels like college hoops."

Knight's teams once won 50 games in a row there. The first full-season Knight recruiting class – the great one that was the nucleus of The Perfect Season team: Quinn Buckner, Scott May, Bobby Wilkerson, Tom Abernethy, Jim Crews – *never* lost a home Big Ten game. In four years.

Eleven Knight teams won Big Ten championships or co-championships; in 75 years of league play before and after Knight, Indiana teams won nine. The NCAA championships came in 1976, '81 and '87, three wholly different rosters. He was in the hunt for a whole lot more. Four other Knight-IU teams were ranked No. 1 at some point of the season, five others No. 2 or 3.

In the summer of 1984, he made Assembly Hall the amateur basketball capital of the world. There, the last great amateur team was picked, then polished into gold-medal shape by Knight and his hand-picked staff of assistants. Michael

Jordan (HOF 2009) lifted that group – which included Patrick Ewing (HOF 2008) – to all-time recognition as the first to draw comparisons with the 1960 team coached by Pete Newell and headed by Oscar Robertson, Jerry West and Jerry Lucas (all, HOF 1980) and Walt Bellamy (HOF 1993). Their unbeaten march to a gold medal at Los Angeles came without Knight ever calling a time out.

Knight also coached the United States to a gold medal at the 1979 Pan American Games. Isiah Thomas and Kevin McHale (HOF 1999) were on that team. He is the only man to coach champions of the NCAA, NIT, Olympic Games, and Pan American Games.

Controversy was an ever-present companion of the hot-tempered Knight, though his victories and championships never were marred by even allegations of an NCAA rules violation, and his players graduated at a near-100 percent rate. A chair he tossed onto the court in anger in 1985 forever branded him. Even at Army, his blow-ups got him the nickname "Bobby T" in the New York press. His superintendent there, and presidents later at Indiana and Texas Tech, repeatedly publicly lauded his academics emphasis, even the one who wound up firing him at

Did You Know?

Women's basketball teams are reduced from six to five players per side with rules for a full court game and the 30-second clock are officially adopted for the **1971-72** season.

Free throws shot after the first six fouls of a half on each team are eliminated in college basketball, and the NCAA declares freshmen eligible to play on varsity teams before the start of the **1972-73** season.

1981-82: Fouls assessed to a team's bench are now credited to the coach.

Indiana in 2000 on his own way to presidency of the NCAA, Myles Brand.

After a season out of basketball (the team he left behind at Indiana played in the 2002 NCAA championship game), Knight returned to coaching at Texas Tech. He inherited a team that had finished last in the Big 12 and coached it to an NCAA tournament berth in his first season and three that came after. It was at the Lubbock school that a 70-68 victory over New Mexico on January 1, 2007, broke his tie with Dean Smith atop the all-time men's major-college victory list. He went on to add 22 more before – with no farewell tour, no fanfare of any kind – he coached his Red Raiders to a 67-60 Saturday win over Oklahoma State, then decided over the weekend and announced on Monday, February 4, 2008, that he was stepping down, immediately. His son and longtime assistant, Pat, bearing the name of the grandfather who couldn't comprehend coaching as a vocational aspiration, took over, as had been long assured.

ESPN signed the 67-year-old Knight as an analyst and commentator, and the record of 902 victories went up as the target for every eager aspirant to shoot for. His one-time Army captain, Krzyzewski – winner of three NCAA championships at Duke and coach of an Olympic champion, too – was first in line as Most Likely. It's not a long line. All you have to do, Coach, is win 30 games in 30 seasons and you'll be just two short. There won't be a lot of chasers.

Year-by-Year Induction Classes

1959

The First Team
Original Celtics
Forrest Clare Allen, Coach *
Henry Clifford Carlson, Coach *
Dr. Luther Gulick, Contributor *
Edward J. Hickox, Contributor *
Charles D. Hyatt, Player *
Matthew P. Kennedy, Referee *
Angelo Luisetti, Player *
Walter E. Meanwell, M.D., Coach *
George L. Mikan, Player *
Ralph Morgan, Contributor *
Dr. James Naismith, Contributor *
Harold G. Olsen, Contributor *
John J. Schommer, Player *
Amos Alonzo Stagg, Contributor *
Oswald Tower, Contributor *

1960

Ernest A. Blood, Coach *
Victor A. Hanson, Player *
George T. Hepbron, Referee *
Frank W. Keaney, Coach *
Ward L. Lambert, Coach *
Edward C. Macauley, Player
Branch McCracken, Player *
Charles C. Murphy, Player *
Henry V. Porter, Contributor *
John R. Wooden, Player +

1961

Buffalo Germans
Bernard Borgmann, Player
Forrest S. DeBernardi, Player *
George H. Hoyt, Referee *
George E. Keogan, Coach *
Robert A. Kurland, Player
John J. O'Brien, Contributor *
Andy Phillip, Player *
Ernest C. Quigley, Referee *
John S. Roosma, Player *
Leonard D. Sachs, Coach *
Arthur A. Schabinger, Contributor*
Christian Steinmetz, Player *
David Tobey, Referee *
Arthur L. Trester, Contributor *
Edward A. Wachter, Player *
David H. Walsh, Referee *

1962

Jack McCracken, Player*
Frank Morgenweck, Contributor*
Harlan O. Page, Player*
Barney Sedran, Player*
Lynn W. St. John, Contributor*
John A. Thompson, Player *

Year-by-Year Induction Classes

1963

New York Rens

Robert F. Gruenig, Player*

William A. Reid, Contributor *

1964

John W. Bunn, Contributor*

Harold E. Foster, Player*

Nat Holman, Player*

Edward S. Irish, Contributor*

R. William Jones, Contributor*

Kenneth D. Loeffler, Coach*

John D. Russell, Player*

1965

Walter A. Brown, Contributor*

Paul D. Hinkle, Contributor*

Howard A. Hobson, Coach*

William G. Mokray, Contributor*

1966

Everett S. Dean, Coach*

Joe Lapchick, Player *

1968

Clair F. Bee, Contributor*

Howard G. Cann, Coach*

Amory T. Gill, Coach*

Alvin F. Julian, Coach *

1969

Arnold J. Auerbach, Coach *

Henry G. Dehnert, Player *

Henry P. Iba, Coach *

Adolph F. Rupp, Coach *

Charles H. Taylor, Contributor *

Patrick Ewing - 2008

Year-by-Year Induction Classes

1970

Bernard L. Carnevale, Coach

Robert E. Davies, Player *

1971

Robert J. Cousy, Player

Robert L. Pettit, Player

Abraham Saperstein, Contributor *

1972

Edgar A. Diddle, Coach *

Robert L. Douglas, Contributor *

Paul Endacott, Player *

Max Friedman, Player *

Edward Gottlieb, Contributor *

W. R. Clifford Wells, Contributor *

1973

John Beckman, Player *

Bruce Drake, Coach *

Arthur C. Lonborg, Coach *

Elmer H. Ripley, Contributor *

Adolph Schayes, Player

John R.Wooden, Coach

1974

Harry A. Fisher, Contributor *

Maurice Podoloff, Contributor *

Ernest J. Schmidt, Player *

1975

Joseph R. Brennan, Player *

Emil S. Liston, Contributor *

William F. Russell, Player

Robert P. Vandivier, Player *

1976

Thomas J. Gola, Player

Edward W. Krause, Player *

Harry Litwack, Coach *

Bill W. Sharman, Player

Larry Bird - 1998

Year-by-Year Induction Classes

1977

Elgin Baylor, Player
Charles T. Cooper, Player*
Lauren Gale, Player*
William C. Johnson, Player*
Frank J. McGuire, Coach*

1978

Paul J. Arizin, Player*
Joseph F. Fulks, Player*
Clifford O. Hagan, Player
John P. Nucatola, Referee*
James C. Pollard, Player*

1979

Justin M. (Sam) Barry, Coach
Wilton N. Chamberlain, Player*
James E. Enright, Referee*
Edgar S. Hickey, Coach*
John B. McLendon, Jr.,
    Contributor*
Raymond J. Meyer, Coach*
Peter F. Newell, Contributor*

1980

Lester Harrison, Contributor*
Jerry R. Lucas, Player
Oscar P. Robertson, Player
Everett F. Shelton, Coach*
J. Dallas Shirley, Referee*
Jerry A. West, Player

1981

Thomas B. Barlow, Player*
Ferenc Hepp, Contributor*
J. Walter Kennedy, Contributor*
Arad A. McCutchan, Coach*

1982

Everett N. Case, Coach*
Alva O. Duer, Contributor*
Clarence E. Gaines, Coach*
Harold E. Greer, Player
Slater N. Martin, Player
Frank V. Ramsey, Jr., Player
Willis Reed, Jr., Player

1983

William W. Bradley, Player
David A. DeBusschere, Player*
Lloyd R. Leith, Referee*
Dean E. Smith, Coach
John (Jack) K. Twyman, Player
Louis G. Wilke, Contributor*

Year-by-Year Induction Classes

Morgan Wootten - 2000

1984

Clifford B. Fagan, Contributor *
James H. (Jack) Gardner, Coach *
John Havlicek, Player
Samuel (Sam) Jones, Player
Edward S. Steitz, Contributor *

1985

Senda Berenson Abbott,
  Contributor *
W. Harold Anderson, Coach *
Alfred N. Cervi, Player
Marv K. Harshman, Coach
Bertha F. Teague, Contributor *
Nate Thurmond, Player
L. Margaret Wade, Coach *

1986

William J. Cunningham, Player
Thomas W. Heinsohn, Player
William "Red" Holzman, Coach *
Zigmund "Red" Mihalik, Referee *
Fred R. Taylor, Coach *
Stanley H. Watts, Coach *

1987

Richard F. Barry, Player
Walter Frazier, Player
Robert J. Houbregs, Player
Peter P. Maravich, Player *
Robert Wanzer, Player

Jerry Colangelo - 2004

Year-by-Year Induction Classes

1988

Clyde E. Lovellette, Player
Robert McDermott, Player*
Ralph H. Miller, Coach*
Westley S. Unseld, Player

1989

William "Pop" Gates, Player*
K. C. Jones, Player
Leonard (Lenny) Wilkens, Player +

1990

David Bing, Player
Elvin E. Hayes, Player
Donald Neil Johnston, Player*
Vernon Earl Monroe, Player

1991

Nathaniel Archibald, Player
David W. Cowens, Player
Lawrence Fleisher, Contributor*
Harry J. Gallatin, Player
Robert M. Knight, Coach
Lawrence F. O'Brien, Contributor*
Borislav Stankovic, Contributor

Jim Calhoun - 2005

1992

Sergei Belov, Player
Louis P. Carnesecca, Coach
Lusia Harris-Stewart, Player
Cornelius L. Hawkins, Player
Robert J. Lanier, Player
Alfred J. McGuire, Coach*
John (Jack) T. Ramsay, Coach
Nera D. White, Player
Phillip D. Woolpert, Coach*

Year-by-Year Induction Classes

Lynette Woodard - 2004

1993

Walter Bellamy, Player
Julius W. Erving, Player
Daniel P. Issel, Player
Ann E. Meyers, Player
Richard S. McGuire, Player
Calvin J. Murphy, Player
Uljana Semjonova, Player
William T. Walton, Player

1994

Carol Blazejowski, Player
Denzil (Denny) E. Crum, Coach
Charles J. Daly, Coach
Harry (Buddy) Jeannette, Player *
Cesare Rubini, Coach

1995

Anne Donovan, Player
Aleksandr Gomelsky, Coach *
Kareem Abdul-Jabbar, Player
John Kundla, Coach
Vern Mikkelsen, Player
Cheryl Miller, Player
Earl Strom, Referee *

Year-by-Year Induction Classes

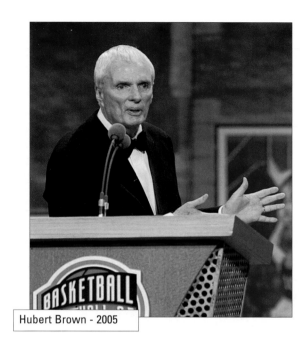

Hubert Brown - 2005

1996

Kresimir Cosic, Player*

George Gervin, Player

Gail Goodrich, Player

Nancy Lieberman, Player

David Thompson, Player

George Yardley, Player*

1997

Pete Carril, Coach

Joan Crawford, Player

Denise Curry, Player

Antonio Diaz-Miguel, Coach*

Alex English, Player

Don Haskins, Coach*

Bailey Howell, Player

1998

Larry Bird, Player

Jody Conradt, Coach

Alexander (Alex) Hannum, Coach*

Marques Haynes, Player

Aleksandar Nikolic, Coach*

Arnold (Arnie) Risen, Player

Leonard (Lenny) Wilkens, Coach+

1999

Wayne Embry, Contributor

Kevin McHale, Player

Billie Moore, Coach

John Thompson, Coach

Fred Zollner, Contributor*

Pat Summit - 2000

Year-by-Year Induction Classes

2000

Danny Biasone, Contributor *
Robert McAdoo, Player
Charles Newton, Contributor
Pat Summitt, Head Coach
Isiah Thomas, Player
Morgan Wootten, Coach

Cathy Rush - 2008

Magic Johnson - 2002

2001

John Chaney, Coach
Mike Krzyzewski, Coach
Moses Malone, Player

2002

Harlem Globetrotters, Team
Larry Brown, Coach
Earvin "Magic" Johnson, Player
Lute Olson, Coach
Drazen Petrovic, Player *
Kay Yow, Coach *

Year-by-Year Induction Classes

2003

Leon Barmore, Coach
Chick Hearn, Contributor*
Meadowlark Lemon, Contributor
Earl Lloyd, Contributor
Dino Meneghin, Player
Robert Parish, Player
James Worthy, Player

2004

Jerry Colangelo, Contributer
Drazen Dalipagic, Player
Clyde Drexler, Player
Bill Sharman, Coach+
Maurice Stokes, Player*
Lynette Woodard, Player

2005

Jim Boeheim, Coach
Hubert "Hubie" Brown, Contributer
Jim Calhoun, Coach
Sue Gunter, Coach*
Hortencia Marcari, Player

2006

Geno Auriemma, Coach
Charles Barkley, Player
Joe Dumars, Player
Sandro Gamba, Coach
David Gavitt, Contributer
Dominique Wilkins, Player

2007

Van Chancellor, Coach
Pedro Ferrandiz, Coach
Phil Jackson, Coach
Mirko Novosel, Coach
Marvin "Mendy" Rudolph, Referee*
Texas Western, Team
Roy Williams, Coach

Charles Barkley - 2006

Year-by-Year Induction Classes

Geno Auriemma - 2006

2009

Michael Jordan, Player
David Robinson, Player
Jerry Sloan, Coach
John Stockton, Player
C. Vivian Stringer, Coach

*Deceased
+Rehonored as a coach

2008

Adrian Dantley, Player
William Davidson, Contributor *
Patrick Ewing, Player
Hakeem Olajuwon, Player
Pat Riley, Coach
Cathy Rush, Coach
Dick Vitale, Contributor

Dick Vitale - 2008

John Bunn Awards

The John Bunn Award is named for the first chairman of the Basketball Hall of Fame Committee (1949-69). The award, instituted by the Basketball Hall's Board of Trustees, annually honors an international or national figure who has contributed greatly to the game of basketball. Outside of Enshrinement, the John Bunn Award is the most prestigious award presented by the Basketball Hall of Fame.

1973	John Bunn	**1992**	Will Robinson
1974	John Wooden	**1993**	Joe Vancisin
1975	J. Walter Kennedy	**1994**	William Wall
1976	Henry P. Iba	**1995**	Pete Carlesimo
1977	Clifford B. Fagan	**1996**	Vic Bubas
1978	Curt Gowdy	**1997**	C.M. Newton
1979	Eddie Gottlieb	**1998**	Tex Winter
1980	Arnold "Red" Auerbach	**1999**	The Harlem Globetrotters
1981	Ray Meyer	**2000**	Meadowlark Lemon
1982	Daniel Biasone	**2001**	Tom Jernstedt
1983	Robert J. Cousy	**2002**	Harvey Pollack
1984	Lawrence F. O'Brien	**2003**	Joe O'Brien
1985	Lee Williams	**2004**	Zelda Spoelstra
1986	Grady W. Lewis	**2005**	Marty Blake
1987	David R. Gavitt	**2006**	Betty Jaynes
1988	Haskell Hillyard	**2007**	Thomas "Satch" Sanders
1989	George E. Killian	**2008**	Val Ackerman
1990	Pat Head Summitt	**2009**	Johnny Kerr
1991	Morgan B. Wootten		

Curt Gowdy Media Awards

The Basketball Hall of Fame's media award is named in honor of Curt Gowdy, who served as president of the Hall of Fame for seven consecutive one-year terms. It was established by the Board of Trustees to single out members of the electronic and print media for outstanding contributions to basketball.

1990 Curt Gowdy, electronic
Dick Herbert, print

1991 Marty Glickman, electronic
Dave Dorr, print

1992 *Chick Hearn, electronic
Sam Goldaper, print

1993 Johnny Most, electronic
Leonard Lewin, print

1994 Cawood Ledford, electronic
Leonard Koppett, print

1995 Dick Enberg, electronic
Bob Hammel, print

1996 Billy Packer, electronic
Bob Hentzen, print

1997 Marv Albert, electronic
Bob Ryan, print

1998 Dick Vitale, electronic
Larry Donald, print
Dick Weiss, print

1999 Bob Costas, electronic
Smith Barrier, print

2000 Hubie Brown, electronic
Dave Kindred, print

2001 Dick Stockton, electronic
Curry Kirkpatrick, print

2002 Jim Nantz, electronic
Jim O'Connell, print

2003 Rod Hundley, electronic
Sid Hartman, print

2004 Max Falkenstien, electronic
Phil Jasner, print

2005 Bill Campbell, electronic
Jack McCallum, print

2006 Bill Raftery, electronic
Mark Heisler, print

2007 Al McCoy, electronic
Malcom Moran, print

2008 Bob Wolf, electronic
David DuPree, print

2009 Doug Collins, electronic
Peter Vecsey, print

Naismith Memorial Basketball Hall of Fame Board of Trustees

Naismith Memorial Basketball Hall of Fame Board of Trustees

The Writers

Ken Dooley met Red Auerbach in 1985 when he wrote and directed the film, "Dedication and Desire: The Red Auerbach Key to Success." A 20-year friendship developed and in 1991, he and Red collaborated on *MBA: Management By Auerbach.* Dooley has published 37 other books and has written and directed more than 80 motivational films. He is currently a senior editor for Progressive Business Publications in Malvern, Pennsylvania.

David DuPree covered the NBA for 30 years during his distinguished career. DuPree played with the Rochester Zeniths of the CBA for half a season for a first-person story for the *Washington Post,* proof that he would do anything to get the story. In 2008, David DuPree was honored with the Naismith Memorial Basketball Hall of Fame's Curt Gowdy Award for print journalism.

Matt Fulks, writer, editor and broadcaster, started his journalism career while attending Lipscomb University in Nashville, Tennessee. He is the author/co-author of 14 books, including *CBS Sports Presents: Stories from the Final Four* and *Echoes of Kansas Basketball.* He also is a regular contributor to various publications, including kcmetrosports.com — the website for Kansas City's all-sports TV station Metro Sports.

Ben Green is the author of four non-fiction books, including *Spinning the Globe: The Rise, Fall and Return to Greatness of the Harlem Globetrotters.* His other books include: *Before His Time, The Soldier of Fortune Murders*, and *Finest Kind.* He lives in Tallahassee, Florida.

The Writers

 Mel Greenberg has been at *The Philadelphia Inquirer* for 40 years, extensively covering women's basketball for 34 years locally and nationally. He is best known for creating what became the Associated Press women's poll. For fostering national coverage of the sport, he has been inducted into the Women's Basketball, Philadelphia Big Five, United States Basketball Writers Association, and Philadelphia Jewish Sports Halls of Fame. Additionally, the Women's Basketball Coaches Association created the Mel Greenberg Media Award in 1991, presenting him with the first honor. The College Sports Information Directors have given him their top media honor — the Jake Wade Award.

 Bob Hammel at 18 covered Oscar Robertson's first state championship in 1955 and grew up in journalism with Indiana high school basketball. He covered 29 state championships in a career that, on his move to the *Bloomington Herald-Telephone* in 1966, shifted emphasis to Indiana University, Big Ten and NCAA athletics, including 23 Final Fours and five Olympics. Author of 11 books, 9 of them basketball-related, in 1996, he received the Naismith Memorial Basketball Hall of Fame's Curt Gowdy Award.

 Blair Kerkhoff, who grew up in ACC country and has covered college sports for *The Kansas City Star* since 1989, couldn't help falling for barbeque and college basketball. Among his books are three on the game's history. On occasion he'll play tour guide, directing visitors to James Naismith's grave site in Lawrence, Kansas.

 Dr. Jim Krause is a lifelong basketball fanatic with an addiction to coaching. He is a 25-year member of the National Association of Basketball Coaches and has coached at all levels from middle school through NCAA Division I. He is a lifetime sports professional who has attended every Final Four since 1973 and has worked for the NABC as Final Four convention staff since 1993. Krause is currently a professional sports consultant with Winning Sports Programs in Seattle. He is the author of *Guardians of the Game: A Legacy of Leadership.*

The Writers

 Jackie MacMullan is a special contributor to ESPN and ESPN.com. She worked for 19 years at the *Boston Globe*, first as a general assignment reporter, then later as an NBA writer, columnist and associate editor. She also covered the NBA for *Sports Illustrated* from 1995-2000. MacMullan has written three books: *Bird Watching* (in collaboration with Larry Bird); *Geno* (in collaboration with Geno Auriemma); and *When the Game Was Ours* (in collaboration with Magic Johnson and Larry Bird). She also appears on Comcast and WHDH-TV in Boston.

 Jack McCallum was a senior writer for 28 years at *Sports Illustrated* and is still a Special Contributor to the magazine, specializing in pro basketball coverage. He is the author of eight books, including the best-selling *Seven Seconds or Less*, about his season with the 2005-06 Phoenix Suns, and a basketball novel, *Foul Lines,* co-written with *SI* colleague Jon Wertheim.In 2005 he was presented the Curt Gowdy Award by the Naismith Memorial Basketball Hall of Fame.

 Jim O'Connell has been the national college basketball writer for The Associated Press since 1987. Jim attended St. John's University and worked as the Sports Information Director at Fordham for two years. He was presented the Curt Gowdy Award by the Naismith Memorial Basketball Hall of Fame in 2002, and is also a member of the U.S. Basketball Writers Association Hall of Fame.

 Terry Pluto is a sports columnist with the *Cleveland Plain Dealer* and the author of more than 20 books on sports, including *Loose Balls: The Short, Wild Life of the American Basketball Association. Sports Illustrated* ranked *Loose Balls* number 13 on its Top 100 Sports Books of All Time. Pluto also co-authored *48 Minutes: A Night in the Life of the NBA* with Bob Ryan.

The Writers

Gary Pomerantz, the author of *WILT, 1962: The Night of 100 Points and the Dawn of a New Era,* and three other books, is a 1982 graduate of the University of California, Berkeley. He wrote on staff for *The Washington Post* during the 1980s and for *The Atlanta Journal-Constitution* during the 1990s. His new book, *The Devil's Tickets: A Night of Bridge, A Fatal Hand & A New American Age,* was released in June 2009.

Bob Ryan joined the *Boston Globe* as a summer intern in 1968, and, aside from a 19-month stay at WCVB, the Boston ABC affiliate, has been there ever since. He covered the Boston Celtics for 13 1/2 years (five championships), and has been a general columnist since 1989. He is a winner of the 1997 Curt Gowdy Award from the Naismith Memorial Basketball Hall of Fame, and is also a member of the USBWA and New England Halls of Fame for his basketball writing. Ryan is the author of 11 books. He has covered many of the major sporting events, including the last nine Olympics, winter and summer. He is the 2000, 2007 and 2008 Sportswriter of the Year, as selected by the National Association of Sportscasters and Sportswriters. He is a frequent contributor to such ESPN programs as the Sports Reporters, Around The Horn and Pardon The Interruption.

Mark Vancil is an award-winning writer. His work has appeared in virtually every major American newspaper including the *New York Times*, *Washington Post*, *Los Angeles Times*, *Chicago Tribune* and *Miami Herald*. He also has written for magazines in North America, Australia and Japan. Mark is President and Principal of Rare Air Media, a Chicago-area publishing and communications company. His new book is *Mystics Among Us*, a look at the critical element that defines, and ultimately separates, icons from superstars across social and political spectrums.

Photo Credits

Steve Lipofsky, basketballphoto.com
Pages: 10, 24a, 24b, 24c, 24d, 28, 30, 32, 34, 52, 55,
84a, 84b, 84d, 84e, 94, 120, 121, 123, 124, 127, 128,
130, 137, 138a, 138b, 138c, 138d, 141a, 141b, 142,
144, 145, 148, 152, 154, 155, 157

Basketball Hall of Fame Properties
Pages: 11, 20a, 20b, 21, 22, 23, 41, 47, 61, 112, 146,
203, 204, 206, 207, 208, 209, 210, 211, 212

David N. Berkwitz/Sports Illustrated
Pages: 66, 68, 69, 72, 73, 74, 75a, 75c, 76, 77, 78, 79,
80, 81, 82e, 83

NBA photos/Getty
Pages: 36a, 36b, 36c, 37a, 37b, 51, 63, 65, 84c,
119, 149, 151, 166, 174

Rich Clarkson and Associates
Pages: 12, 38, 100, 136, 171, 177

Mike Strauss, Switch
Pages: 75b, 75d, 82a, 82b, 82c, 82d

Associated Press
Pages: 64, 132, 150

Rutgers University Sports Information
Pages: 24e, 26, 37c

University of Kansas
Pages: 43, 44, 49, 190

University of Kentucky
Page: 54b

Louisiana State University
Page: 54a

Archival Images
Pages: 40, 42, 89

Aerial Photography by Don Couture
Pages: 70-71

John Molina
Page: 60

Photos courtesy of respective writers
Authors, pages 218-222

**Cover and Dust Jacket courtesy of Basketball Hall
of Fame Properties**

Acknowledgements

Ascend Books gratefully acknowledges the contributions of the following individuals to the success of *Hoops Heaven*:

To John Doleva, Don Senecal, Scott Zuffelato, and Paul Lambert, of the Naismith Memorial Basketball Hall of Fame - our thanks for your support of and commitment to this exciting project. You put the ball in play!

To Matt Zeysing, Historian and Archivist - Thanks for your help with writing, editing, and co-managing the project. Thanks for your full-court press!

To Steve Lipofsky, who rained great photos like 15-foot jumpers - thanks!

Our appreciation to key players in the design, editing and printing process including Cindy Ratcliff, Bob Audley, Mark McCombs, and Randy Lackey. Special thanks as well to Miles Schnaer who provided some great coaching along the way.

And to everyone else who had an assist with this project - you're stars in our book!